The Language of Success

The Language of Success

An Interpreter's Entrepreneurial Journey

Theresa Slater

ıılıBEP

BUSINESS EXPERT PRESS Q

Leader in applied, concise business books

The Language of Success: An Interpreter's Entrepreneurial Journey

Copyright © Business Expert Press, LLC, 2025

Cover design by Stefan Prodanovic

Interior design by Exeter Premedia Services Private Ltd., Chennai, India

First published in 2024 by
Business Expert Press, LLC
222 East 46th Street, New York, NY 10017
www.businessexpertpress.com

ISBN-13: 978-1-63742-620-3 (paperback)
ISBN-13: 978-1-63742-621-0 (e-book)

Business Expert Press Business Career Development Collection

First edition: 2024

10 9 8 7 6 5 4 3 2 1

I dedicate this book to my 15-year-old self. Thrown totally unprepared into a world that was often dangerous and constantly threatening. Living hand to mouth, navigating crisis to crisis instead of navigating high school and living my best teenage life. Who, at 15, never could have envisioned success further than food in her mouth and a roof over her head.

Success is not built on success. It's built on failure. It's built on frustration. Sometimes it's built on catastrophe.

—Sumner Redstone

Description

From the street smarts of a 15-year-old rose a triumphant entrepreneur whose resilience and determination forged a path to success. The Language of Success is a story of survival, self-improvement, and accomplishment.

In these pages, the author walks us through her sometimes-tumultuous upbringing in a "milky-white" town of little diversity, while striving to understand the bigger world around her. From leaving home at 15 and facing daily challenges of survival, to finding those paths to nontraditional education and opportunities—this unorthodox route into the world of business and later linguistics showcases the opportunities and "go with your guts" intuition that often lead to places you never dreamed of.

The lessons learned through years of minimum wage jobs and struggle were later her building blocks for success. Over the course of two decades, she built her company, Empire Interpreting Service, into a leading language service provider (LSP). Theresa bootstrapped her company and molded it into a respected, award-winning organization that has been cited as the "gold standard" in its field.

Keywords

language service provider; interpreting; street smarts; entrepreneurs; small business; American sign language; freelancing; request for proposal; networking; languages; employees; female business owner; boards; memberships; promoting; interpreter; bootstrapping; small business advice

Contents

Testimonials

"Theresa's story is very inspiring, and a must read for anyone looking to follow their dream and start a business. The work she's done with Empire Interpreting Service has helped so many across the globe and, as the leader of a woman-owned business, she has succeeded with perseverance, drive and purpose."—**Stephen Fournier KeyBank, President, Central New York Market**

"Thank you for sharing The Language of Success with me. I find the personalization angle very impactful. You are giving voice to what many potential entrepreneurs go through with impostor syndrome and self-doubt. The narrative about your dad, his impact and the part he played in your origin story was amazing. The "lesson" at the end of each section is wonderful, whether it is customer service, employee care or guerilla marketing, they were all fantastic.

I am currently teaching a course through Syracuse University titled Foundations of Entrepreneurship for people with disabilities. If this book was available, I would assign it as required reading."—**John Liddy, CEO, Innovation and Entrepreneurship, Instructor, Whitman School of Business, Syracuse University**

"The Language of Success is a story that needs to be told! You sharing your personal journey is inspiring and can help others who feel they are alone in their journey from starting at below the bottom to being successful. It can even be an inspiration for those thinking they will not make it. Your "Aha!" moment (of recognizing the needs of your interpreters), was thought provoking. Most businesspeople do not think of the workers' needs, you are different. This is going to be a great book for people contemplating starting their own business as well as people who are at the top feeling they are the only ones out there alone.

Life taught you some life lessons for sure, lessons of resourcefulness, lessons of how to not forget where you came from, and most importantly, how to love/care for yourself so that you can care for others!

And I wish I had security footage of you in the Wegmans Beer cooler!"
—**Susan Freeman, Interpreter Services, SUNY Upstate Medical University**

Acknowledgments

I would first like to thank my sons, Jay and Trevor, who continued to support my dream while they put their own aspirations on hold. The fact that through working with me, we are in daily communication with each other has truly been a blessing. And to the contributions they made to the company, from Jay's vision to build a software platform that ran the company, to Trevor's foresight of needing and building a social media network. I am forever grateful.

I'd also like to thank my CFO, Stacey Short, who came to me as my first hire and whose loyalty, friendship, and work ethic are unsurpassed. I will always be grateful for her being in my life. And for Corissa Hedrick, who came to me almost 20 years ago straight out of college and had the drive and ambition to build a spoken language department at Empire Interpreting Service (EIS). Watching both young women grow in their business and personal lives into competent, polished businesswomen has been incredibly rewarding.

And to those first six interpreters listed on the laminated card who you will learn were the catalyst for my business. These are the individuals I had such respect and trust in that I knew could help change the way the language service industry was run: Amy Lynne, Dinah Decker, Ginger Fairbanks, Amy Sakellariou, Virginia Scarpino, and Mareike Larsen.

And lastly to my editor, Vilma Barr, who heard my story and thought it worth telling. Her encouragement and guidance along the way pushed me to have the courage to tell the parts of my journey I had kept hidden for decades. And to be bold enough to be proud of the outcome.

CHAPTER 1

Roots in a "Milky White" Town

I think I have a unique history. I think knowing it would help you understand me better and how my personal life journey shaped the future journey of my business.

I was born in Central New York State, My parents were loving, and our world was very family focused. My mother was a stay-at-home mom. I had an older sister and a younger brother. Shortly before I left home at 15, another little brother came along.

Our small town of about 20,000 was what my mom called "milky white," a term I did not hear until my parents decided to become foster parents. Since our family was no longer 100 percent white, I guess, the rest of the town looked "milky white." We also became overnight targets of curiosity and misunderstanding at the least, to racism and bullying, at the worst, which I think played a lot into my eventual desire to expand my life beyond the four corners of my small hometown.

I became pregnant as a result of a rape at 15. When the administrators at my high school found out, they decided it best I leave the beginning of my sophomore year so as not to be a bad example to other students that might see me in the hall with a baby bump.

I never told my parents about the rape. They assumed it was from a friendship with a 17-year-old boy I had just started seeing, a senior at my high school. Marriage to him was the answer to the embarrassment of my condition. I lost the baby in my fifth month, a week before the wedding. The wedding happened the following week anyway.

These things are important as you might suspect because I was on my own at 15, without a high school education and with a 17-year-old husband. He had been raised in a not-so-loving home and was surrounded by alcoholism and violence. His past spilled over into my life for the next seven years. By the age of 22, I had been married for seven years, had a three-year-old, and was divorced. Again, on my own. And again, I did not tell my parents of what I had been facing daily.

All these things affected how I looked at myself and how I looked at the world. While my peers were attending college and going to homecoming parties, I was maneuvering crisis after crisis. Always in survival mode and with zero sense of self or self-confidence. I felt less than, dumber than, a poor uneducated townie. My parents were not poor or uneducated. People loved and respected them. I had not come from the wrong side of the tracks. Circumstances had dictated where I was in life. Fortunately, outside of being in survival mode, I was constantly in self-improvement mode. How I pulled out of this existence is another story, but this part needs to be told so that anyone reading the following business advice tidbits understands how I looked at things and how I got from A to Z.

CHAPTER 2

To All Entrepreneurs

While I believe my journey and my stories throughout this book will resonate with female entrepreneurs, my hope is that any small business owner would read this book and relate. I have learned from women and men alike over the years, having many "Aha" moments and finding advice I never knew I needed.

That is my hope that you, the reader, will find moments you relate to: moments you have faced and moments you will face in the future. My journey from a 15-year-old out on her own with only a ninth grade education to a successful business owner that puts millions of dollars a year into our economy and puts hundreds of interpreters to work each year—it's not so much rags-to-riches as it is a story of street smarts and how to access information, advice, and support throughout your journey.

For women, this journey can take on many unique challenges. From hiring family to juggling family. From the little girl inside wanting everyone to like them and not rock the boat, to negotiating contracts, to juggling the care of elderly parents while babysitting some of your employees. It must all be done and will be done. It's the advice, support, and knowledge that help you get through and not to have a disaster on your hands.

Male or female, business owners will need support, guidance, and resources. We will need family, friends, and professionals to come beside us. We will need to constantly educate ourselves, not only on leadership but on our industry, technology, the stock market, world affairs, and government policies, all of which affect us growing our businesses.

We need to know how to choose everything from a computer to a CPA. We must know how to move through the stages of startup, when you do everything yourself, to hiring staff, and then how to pull yourself away from the revenue-producing role to the strategic thinker. We need to know how to take care of ourselves physically and mentally and how to have boundaries.

There is no one book or MBA degree to teach you this. As you'll read in this book, there were so many situations no one could have ever prepared me for. From walking in on someone supergluing their dentures to having one of my managers shoo mice out of the way so they wouldn't interrupt a contract negotiation. You can't make this stuff up, but it is the real life of a business owner.

For me, it was learning how to survive on my own at 15 and trying to calculate how to get enough food for the week, to having successes I could never have dreamed of. I knew what it was like to struggle. I honestly wasn't prepared to handle successes. However, somehow out of all that survival via street smarts, decades later, came true success.

CHAPTER 3

First Signs of Success

The first time I truly stopped and thought "You've arrived!" was in a Wegmans grocery store. I had run in on a mad dash between work and going to visit my mother in her assistive living facility—some things my mom needed, some items I needed. I hurried to the check out with a cart full of items and realized as I handed over my debit card that I never put any thought into how much this shopping trip was going to cost. I stopped halfway through handing the card to the cashier and said to myself, *"this doesn't even matter."* How surreal that moment felt. I knew whatever it was, I could afford it. My first sign of success.

This was in stark contrast to most of my life, coupons in one hand and a handheld calculator in the other, making sure I didn't exceed what I had in my checking account. More times than I can count, items were put back before I reached the checkout because I was over limit. And then there were the really tough times of being a single mom, when a box of Cheerios and a package of hotdogs were carefully calculated, all in order to see how many meals I could get out of each item. Working three minimum-wage jobs simultaneously and scheduling "chance" visits to my grandparents or my parents around dinner time. This strategy paid off as it filled in other nights when dinner for my son would have been difficult if not impossible.

My family in its entirety had taught us growing up that there was no shame in being poor. Although they were not poor, they had all had times of struggle they had gone through. My grandmother had been poor and lived through the Great Depression. Her advice was to "stay clean, have your clothes pressed and presentable, be kind and considerate, and be respectful," as if doing all that meant you somehow escaped the stressors of being poor. Present yourself to the world as if everything was alright. Never ask for handouts or help. Never. Have pride: work, work, work. And, if you were a woman, you add on the responsibilities of a perfect home. Be a perfect wife; have perfect children. These were another generation's signs of success.

So fast forward to today. My business turned 20 years old in 2023. I now employ staff to run the company while utilizing the services of hundreds of interpreters and translators at any given time. Both of my sons work for me, which means I have the satisfaction of knowing that building my business has helped them build their careers. Empire Interpreting Service (EIS) is known for its excellence, and we were presented with the Small Business of the Year award by the Small Business Association for the state of New York. I am very proud of my business and our standards are high. That is what I call signs of business success.

I live in a beautiful condo in downtown Philadelphia, and I drive a nice car. I am regularly going on vacations for the first time in my life. I can help friends and family and contribute to causes I feel a kinship with when it's needed. I can afford things I never thought I would in the first four decades of my life. That's the financial success. But what still resonates with me is every trip to the grocery store, where I put whatever I want in the cart, and don't think about the cost. And I no longer must count out how many hotdogs in a package will feed my son that week.

And it all began with a 15-year-old standing at the back of a church ... readying herself to walk down the aisle.

CHAPTER 4

The Wedding

My grandfather stood in his Sunday best. Tall and handsome, he stoically seemed to guard the side door of the church's Interfaith Chapel. It was mid-November and cold in upstate New York. The mixture of rain and snow slowly ran over his hat and down the back of his overcoat. A collective and quiet man, this was a statement to my family of major proportions. He was *outside*. Earlier that day, he affirmed to my grandmother that he would not watch his granddaughter being "led like a lamb to the altar." He stayed outside like a silent guard to the innocence that was about to be broken on the inside of the church.

To this day, I wish someone would have saved that little lamb and pulled her from the altar she was about to approach.

I stood at the back of the church, in a short wedding gown and veil that my mother had found at a sample sale. Everything had been done quickly. Quietly. And it seemed the expectation was that everyone at the wedding would follow suit and act as if this were somehow normal. I was 6 months and 16 days past my 15th birthday when I walked down the aisle to meet my soon to be 17-year-old husband. Nothing about this was normal.

This was the beginning of what would mold me. A future that would force me to survive independently of the safe and loving home I was about to exit. A bird pushed out of the nest who was about to either learn how to fly on her own or crash. I did both.

At 15, the instinct of survival was about to kick in. Outside of babysitting the neighborhood kids, I had never had a job. Now, a job was a matter of a roof over my head and food in my stomach. My teenage husband was still in high school, working part time at a local grocery after classes. This was far from what we needed for rent and groceries. My hunt for work was on.

I realized quickly that the one place no one asked for working papers was restaurants. In an attempt to look older, I pulled my long black hair back and off my shoulders. I applied heavy makeup. I lied about my age. I lied about my experience as a waitress and my first job was secured. (It was my first lesson in "fake it until you make it"—more about that later.) I took the noon-to-8 p.m. shift because I was told if you worked during meal hours, your food was free. This meant six days a week I would be receiving two free meals, my first lesson in being resourceful.

I was a good waitress. A *really good* waitress. I came to work early, my uniform clean and pressed, my hair neatly in place, and I was willing to do whatever my co-workers needed. I would help the busboys, dishwashers, and other wait staff. I took over the grill when the cooks went for a cigarette break. I volunteered to clean the bathrooms and the booths when no one else wanted to. I was so afraid of losing this minimum-wage job that I was frantically jumping in everywhere. What I didn't know was that I was living a model I would eventually frame my business after: the horizontal business model.

I would major in minimum-wage jobs over the next several years. From each, I learned a lesson of what worked and didn't work in businesses and unknowingly carried them into my own business decades later. For each of those jobs, I will forever be grateful.

CHAPTER 5

Hometown, Rural Central NY

I grew up on the outskirts of Cortland, a small rural town in upstate New York with a population of 19,000. Cortland is 30 miles south of Syracuse and 45 miles north of Binghamton. In the 1950s and 1960s, it was a prosperous town filled with manufacturing firms: Smith Corona typewriters, Brockway trucks, and the Wickwire Company, makers of metal wire products.

The norm in the community when I was growing up was that you graduated high school and immediately went to work at one of the local manufacturing businesses. Even though the State University of New York: Cortland (SUNY Cortland) had been a mainstay of the community since the early 1800s, few locals were attending the college when I grew up. There was a clear delineated line of "Cortland townies," which meant the uneducated locals, and the "SUNY elites," those who worked at or attended as students.

Cortland is cold. The yearly average temperature is 56 degrees and it averages 85 inches of snow per year. The seasons dictate a wild fluctuation of highs and lows, with a record high of 100 degrees Fahrenheit and a record low of 32 below. If you love the country and the changes of the seasons, it can be a beautiful place to live, with crisp air and crunchy snow mountains in the winter and green, lush fields in the summer. However, Cortland was a challenge to live in—driving in brutal winter weather, constantly fighting the wind and snow, and frustratingly too short summers.

With little expectations for kids to attend college, it also limited our view of the world. Due to the limited diversity of races, I don't remember seeing an African American in the town of Cortland until I saw a three-day-old infant laid in my mother's arms when my parents became foster parents.

CHAPTER 6

Foster Parents

I believe my parents' decision to become foster parents was my first desire to know more about the world outside of our small industrial town in upstate New York. My parents had tried to have a fourth child for several years and when my mom did become pregnant, only to deliver a premature and stillbirth baby, she was devastated. I'm not sure how my parents came to the decision to foster newborns, but I am sure it was connected to losing that baby.

This was pre-*Roe v. Wade* and abortion was still illegal. That meant there was an abundance of need to place newborns into adoptive homes and the need for families to foster those newborns until they were placed into their permanent families. Unlike what you see in a TV show, the beautiful newborns were not handed into the arms of a waiting couple at birth. They were placed into my mother's arms and then stayed in the wicker bassinet she had so carefully readied until the adoption agency decided where they would be permanently placed.

While this filled a need I believe my mother had to care and nurture a newborn, it also brought unwanted side effects into our home. My first realization of that was when my parents sat my brother, sister, and me on the couch for a family meeting. We always knew that meant some important information was about to be delivered or one of us was in trouble! My parents explained that the adoption agency had called and asked if my parents would be willing to foster a baby of color. I didn't realize what that really meant. What was the difference? A baby was a baby, right? And that's what my parents had told the social worker. Of course, they would care for any baby that needed a home. What I didn't realize was what was left unspoken: what this might mean for us as a family and for us individually.

Babies came and went and soon a baby of color was placed in my mother's arms. Like all babies, she had a handmade bunting, designed, and crafted by my grandmother, waiting for her, along with a bassinet which would stay by my parents' bedside until the baby was old enough to move to the nursery. However, the first time my mother loaded us and the new baby into the car to do our weekly grocery shopping and errands, I was to see what my parents had tried to prepare us for when they had gathered us on the couch for our family meeting.

My mother wrapped the baby carefully in her bunting and placed her in a carriage, which she took into the local drug store to pick up a few things. It was then I heard a man walk by, look at the baby, and say to my mother words I didn't yet understand, but made my mother tear up. She nestled the baby in her arms, left her shopping, and hurried us to the car. I really didn't understand what had happened until years later. But I knew it had something to do with our new little sister.

Things escalated from that incident to my brother and me being told to now sit at the back of the school bus by the bus driver. Once the word got out a black baby was in our house, racism crept into our young lives. My little brother would be bullied and beaten up by other kids. I was constantly defending him, angry and not understanding what we had done wrong. At a holiday get-together, I overheard a family member whisper my mother was now a "Foster Mammy." Everything in my nine-year-old body wanted to scream out. Why was something so loving being mocked by people who did not even live in my house?

Things escalated when the pastor at our church took my dad aside one Sunday morning and relayed his concern of "what others would think" about my mother as she walked through town with these babies of color. I saw my dad's face redden before he quickly ushered us all outside.

That sunny summer morning after his conversation with the pastor, he sat us down on the warm church side lawn, in a semicircle, under a large oak tree, and placed the baby in her perfect pink bunting in the middle of us. "This is your little sister. She is innocent and needs our love and protection until she goes to her permanent Mommy and Daddy. That means going forward this is not a safe place for her. You need to know why we will not be coming back." My Dad was a trustee of the church at that time. My mother was a Girl Scout leader whose troop held weekly meetings in the church. I had no idea at that time how much they must have given up in friendships and community for these little babies who would only be with us for a few weeks or months.

Those few years my parents were foster parents to newborns were wonderful and precious, especially for my mom. Yet, the whispers and often not-so-quiet judgments were at times heartbreaking for the family and especially hard on us kids. We were suddenly mini protectors of what is right and good. We felt responsible for fighting for not only these babies, but anyone we deemed an underdog.

It left a lasting impression on the three of us and, I believe, carried into decisions we all made going forward into our adulthood. We knew what white privilege was before the phrase was ever coined. We understood that standing up for what's right would mean paying a price, before we were even teenagers. It made me respect, love, and admire our parents for their decisions while simultaneously resenting them for making our lives so much more difficult.

The climatic end to my parents' fostering newborns came with Jill. My sister had named her. Each baby placed in our care came with a letter of the alphabet, and we were to give each child a temporary name beginning with the designated letter. My parents allowed us to take turns giving the babies a name. Jill lived with us for 13 months. She was a biracial baby and deemed "difficult to place" (remember, this was the 1960s), but by this time, she truly was our little sister. More importantly, my parents were "Mama" and "Dada" to her. They decided to start the paperwork to adopt her permanently. They were ultimately rejected as Jill was deemed "too dark," and us "too white," to call her our own.

The day the social worker came a few weeks later to place Jill with her permanent adoptive "Black enough" parents, she screamed for my parents as they placed her in the car. The social worker took her beautiful newborn bunting my grandmother had made a year prior, her favorite stuffed toy, and her baby book my mother had religiously kept, as she had for each of the babies, and piled them all into the backseat of her waiting car.

It was the first time I had ever seen my father cry. He stood by our picture window looking at the scene in the driveway. His little girl being carried away with her arms outstretched, crying for him. He turned to my mother and said sternly, *"Never again, Dorothy, never again!"* That was the last baby to come into our home. I blamed my parents for letting those people take my little sister away and would not speak to them for days. I remained in my bedroom and refused to come out to eat, watch TV, or play. My parents finally took me to a family friend who talked to me and tried to make me understand what had happened.

Thinking back now, I wonder if she was some kind of therapist. Regardless, the lesson that life was not fair had not escaped me. The knowledge I gained that day was that my parents had really fought hard for Jill at a great cost. I left my room and slowly opened up again. It occurs to me today that I had a blind eye as to what my sister and brother were also experiencing, but today, I can only imagine the pain it caused them as well. My sister was obviously impacted as she named her only daughter Jill.

It was a scant few years between Jill leaving us and my leaving home.

CHAPTER 7

A Child Bride

The marriage was untenable for both me and my teenage husband. Our backgrounds clashed, our outlook on life clashed, and our emotions clashed daily. I believe our marriage would have ended much sooner had it not been for the letter that one day came from the U.S. Military. Your number is "…" and you held your breath that your number was close to 366, the top number, and not a low number, as these young men were drafted first. When my young husband's number came up in the low 20s, he knew a draft notice was imminent. The war in Vietnam was still raging on. A draft notice was viewed as a death notice by all who received one.

We were told that if your number came in low, to enlist as soon as possible. Enlistment meant that you at least had a say in which arm of the military you would serve and a possible choice of where you would be stationed. We sat in the recruitment office and looked at a long list of bases where we would live for the next 12 months, after basic and advanced individualized training (AIT). He was to pick his top three choices and one would be awarded. Friends told him to put his top choice as #3. We were teenagers and saw California on the list. We envisioned a beautiful beach and living near the ocean, so California became our #3 choice. And our friends were right—California became our home immediately after his basic training and AIT were complete.

For two years, I had been a child bride of 15, 16, and now 17. This was the first time I had ever been on an airplane. I was leaving the security of being near family and traveling 3,000 miles away to Fort Ord, California, to be with my "soldier-husband" and start a life totally foreign to me in a place where I knew no one, far away from my safety net.

We ended up staying in California throughout the remainder of his military career. While we were there, President Nixon announced the end of military involvement in Vietnam and young soldiers were to remain wherever they were stationed until the end of their commitment.

We were lucky enough to be living in Monterey, California, a beautiful small beachfront town with breathtaking views and pristine weather. It was there I had my first son and there, I was exposed to the Monterey Language Institute. Then called the Presidio of Monterey, the renamed Army Language School was established to meet the requirements of America's global commitments during the Cold War. Instructors, including native speakers of more than 30 languages and dialects, were recruited from all over the world. Soldiers were sent to the Presidio to learn the language and culture of countries to which they would eventually be deployed.

Seeing the many national flags flying in front of the Presidio was always a stirring sight. Walking past on trips to the beach, with my son in his carriage, I would hear the different languages being spoken in and outside of the buildings. It was fascinating. It was invigorating. Just like the babies in my mother's arms, it was a reminder that there were other worlds outside my door. After five years of being a teenage wife and mother, anything outside my door felt like a waiting and welcome escape.

CHAPTER 8

The Big Escape

My first marriage inevitably ended. I was 22, divorced, and with a three-year-old. I moved back to New York to be near my family. I obtained a job in a car dealership as a receptionist and then later as their title clerk. I honestly don't remember the interview. I do think my father being well known in town and a general manager for a local car dealership may have swayed them into hiring me. I'm not sure. But, I was there and making enough money for the first time working just one job in order to pay bills and buy groceries. I still depended on those drop-in visits with family, strategically timed around dinner time, to fill in my meal planning for myself and my son. But, I was scraping by on my own while still looking for ways to better our lives.

That opportunity came within the car dealership I was working for. The office manager had become ill and needed to take an extended leave. Her job consisted of payroll, accounts receivable/payable, and producing a monthly financial statement—none of which I knew anything about. Luckily for me, the dealership had a young, fresh-faced accountant who came up with the idea of training me to fill in for the office manager while she was out. He could "easily train me," he announced, which would save the owners a lot of money versus bringing in someone new. This was a franchised Datsun–Saab dealership and was offering a free one-year program in business management directed specifically at car dealerships. Between working with the CPA and attending the business management classes, I was on my way to taking a big step up in my role at work and business education.

The program I attended was hyperfocused on the car industry—from parts and service to sales, finance and insurance (F&I), and reading financial statements. Although I had learned how to plug numbers in to produce a profit and loss (P&L) or balance sheet, to really understand what those numbers meant in terms of running a business was eye opening. I finally understood what a healthy profit margin was and how to calculate the true cost of sales. I started to worry about accounts receivable and how we were going to make payables, something I never would have even given a thought to preceding my business class.

Instead of just reporting to work and receiving a paycheck, I was now fascinated by how a business should run. Why was it important to look at the business as a whole and from the top down? I began to get hungry for more knowledge.

CHAPTER 9

Moving Forward

A few years later, I met my second husband, also working in the car business. I had since left the first dealership that had sent me to the business school. I had been lured away by a bigger paycheck and better title. The showroom full of Datsuns and Saabs was now replaced by a showroom of Pontiacs and Buicks.

It was here Bob and I met. He was fresh out of college and a representative of the town's stark dividing line I grew up with. I was a townie, worse yet, an uneducated townie, divorced with a 5-year-old, and only 24. We really didn't like each other much when we met. He had been a national athlete throughout his college career and I saw him as a BMOC (big man on campus) total jock type. We had nothing in common.

Regardless, our co-workers were constantly pushing us together. We ended up in a group that met weekly for card games and became good friends. Good friends turned into a very fast romance when my grandfather died. Bob was very kind and sensitive to what I was going through—losing the first person in my young life that I loved, while I was trying to keep it together being a single mom working through my grief. He would come over to my apartment and take me and my son to the park or out for ice cream. And one summer night, he invited us to a drive-in movie. That was when I first fell in love.

As I readied the inside of the car for the movie by getting out the popcorn, soda, and blankets, I caught a glimpse of him playing catch with a small football my son had brought with him. Watching them interact and seeing the kindness and gentleness he exuded gave me a sense of peace and safety I hadn't known since I left home almost nine years earlier. I was exhausted from the struggles. I was hungry for someone to provide me with security. And I was a bit in awe that this college graduate and world-class athlete was so interested in someone like me.

We were married within a year of that first date. And the following year, I had my second son.

We struggled financially and had relationship issues on and off, but I had a husband who was kind and good to my sons. Our family was whole and loving, and the marriage lasted for decades. What I couldn't see coming was that my future success as a business owner would have an unexpected side effect of gaining self-worth and self-esteem, something that eventually reframed my thinking about what I needed and deserved.

Prior to my success, I only knew I didn't "measure up" and that I would do anything to try to be good enough. To me, that included proving that I could be financially successful. To get there, I had to, at some point, get out of survival mode and realize I needed a formal education along with what I'd learned on the job. It was only because of an illness that I was finally motivated enough to push through my fear of becoming a nontraditional student and finish my education. *I was determined to not die without a college degree.*

CHAPTER 10

I Can't Die Without a Degree

It took almost exactly a year to battle the demon. From the first day of poisoning my body in order to eradicate the intruder crawling within, to the last day where I could begin to build myself back up.

I had secretly obtained my GED years previously, in between my many minimum-wage jobs. Now, to keep my mind off the radiation and chemotherapy treatments, I decided to pursue my love of languages and fast-tracked my undergraduate degree in cultural studies with a secondary in interpreting. Life was now in hyperdrive; everything became a drama, and unreasonable fear seemed to rule the day, hour by hour. I reasoned that if I "hurried up" my studies, I could at least leave the legacy to my children that I had a college degree (one of my many fears was the fear that I would die without letters behind my name, thereby embarrassing my surviving family). And so, I vowed to finish my degree at the same time my treatments were completed. Within 12 months. And I almost succeeded.

Another opportunity for self-improvement was discovered, through Empire State College. A State University of New York college, they offered multiple ways to earn credits through traditional and nontraditional classes. One was gaining credit for verifiable university-level learning and life experience gained outside a traditional classroom. I began working with a counselor at the school, gathering transferrable credits I had gained at different colleges and testing out of classes due to my life experiences. While going through medical treatments, I was able to complete my BS in cultural studies with a minor in interpreting for the deaf. Simultaneously, I was working on prepping and sitting for my national certification through RID (Registry of Interpreters for the Deaf), which included a mixture of classes, internships, and work experience.

I received my certification in 18 months and received my permission to stop treatments and resume a normal life. Surprisingly, both events were almost anticlimactic. Life was a little surreal during that time of *picking myself up and looking around the universe* to decide what would follow. Everything was eerily quiet, and I could not find a playbook for "after cancer," so I tried to decipher what I'd learned through it all.

What I *had* learned throughout these crazy 18 months was that I had fallen in love with my chosen language of study, American Sign Language, and the culture that it was woven into. Consequently, I chose to start my interpreting career as an independent freelance interpreter, which took me to a place 10 years later that would put that love and experience to good use. Along with my established love for business and newfound love for linguistics, I decided to start a business. I felt I could do it bigger and better: EIS—Empire Interpreting Service. But, first, my tenure as a freelancer.

CHAPTER 11

Work as a Freelancer

Freelance sign language interpreters will work for one or more agencies known as "language service providers." I signed up with three different agencies. Living in Central New York gave me the opportunity to travel to each corner of the state and provide services to a multitude of consumers. Consumers are the individuals needing interpreting services. If you are trying to communicate with someone that does not share your language, you are technically both consumers.

The assignments varied from academic settings, from kindergarten through postsecondary, to medical, business, and legal work. I loved the

Figure 11.1 My first assignment as a freelance interpreter, working with a 5th grader

variety, and I didn't even mind the 25,000 miles per year I was putting on my car. I was being paid for my time in the car and took advantage of it by listening to everything I could get my hands on relating to linguistics or business. Being a freelancer *is* having your own business. YOU are your business and I wanted to learn as much as I could about how to do this right, which also led to lessons I'd learn for my future business.

There are so many fascinating stories that came about because of my time working as a freelancer. We are present when people come into the world and when they leave this world. Our hands tell our consumers the best and the worst news of their lives. We stand next to the famous and the infamous. We are the first peek a deaf preschooler gets to learning what language means. And it is how a Cornell MBA student learns how to run a business.

CHAPTER 12

Carpal Tunnel and Colonoscopies

As I mentioned, interpreters are often in places you would never be allowed in, or want to be in during your life. Some are fascinating, some heartbreaking, and some exciting. Interpreters often find themselves in medical situations, as this is such a big part of the requests that come in.

On one such assignment, a deaf woman was going in for carpal tunnel surgery. It has been reported that 59 percent of sign language communicators have some kind of wrist/hand problems due to overuse syndrome. Hence, this was not an unusual scenario. What was unusual was when the surgeon stopped talking to the patient, turned to me, and asked, "Would you like to observe the surgery?" It is always a bit startling when you're in the middle of interpreting and one of the consumers looks to you and addresses you directly. I stopped momentarily and before I had a chance to reply, the deaf patient signed to me, "Sure, go ahead! That would be cool for you to observe." She was having the surgery in the same surgical suite with only a local anesthesia and so I stayed. It was not only fascinating, but also a reminder to me that as a professional sign language interpreter, I needed to be careful to protect myself from overuse situations, such as working for long periods solo or not warming up before interpreting. My aversion to anything "gory" was overtaken by my curiosity and the patient's excitement that I be in the room with her. A cool experience for sure!

Another unforgettable experience was with a deaf patient going in for a routine colonoscopy. Again, I assumed that after the nurses were done prepping her and the doctor was done explaining the procedure, I would be left to wait next to the empty gurney while the procedure was completed. As they started to roll away the patient, the doctor doing the procedure motioned for me. "Get masked and gowned up. I need you in the room!"

I'm sure the look of horror on my face said it all. He followed up by explaining that during the procedure they will sometimes ask the patient to turn over, and even though they are under anesthesia (commonly known as "twilight sleep"), they are able to follow instructions. He wanted me there to sign with her if they needed her to turn. I hesitated, not having time to ask the patient herself if it was agreeable to her that I was in the room, but the doctor insisted. I still had no idea how she would "see" my directions if under anesthesia. Again, the consumer said, "Come on in with me. It'll be a cool experience!" But it was definitely nothing like the carpal tunnel surgery I had observed before.

I spent the next half hour in the far corner of the procedure room, in the dark, avoiding the screen on the wall that showed the probe fishing through this woman's colon. The doctor never needed me for any instruction; however, he repeatedly asked me to look at the screen because he evidently thought this was just an awesome opportunity for me to get an up-close and personal view of a colonoscopy. It wasn't. And when I was old enough to need a colonoscopy, I put it off for four years because of the day I stood in that dark corner gowned up from head to foot, trying to avoid what I knew someday I would be experiencing.

CHAPTER 13

Working in the Dark

One of the reasons I ended up starting my own company was the lack of information we would receive in the field as interpreters regarding our assignments. Often, we only had a date, time, and address. We were walking into most assignments in the dark, not knowing what to expect.

One of those times was at the home of a young deaf couple. I was only told there was to be a "meeting" and that some of their family would be involved. I did not know they had a young child who was around three years old. He was hearing and when I knocked on the door, he was the one who answered. His parents did not have the flashing light doorbell that is common in deaf households. He was the one to answer the door as he was the one who could hear the knock.

I looked around the apartment. It was meticulously clean. It seemed small and unusually sparse of furnishings. I later learned that was intentional due to the mom's condition. I saw nowhere we could sit for any type of meeting. As I looked around, the dad led me to another arm of the apartment and to a kitchen table to wait for the person who would run our meeting, and I quickly engaged in conversation with the three-year-old. He suddenly jumped up as a middle-aged man with a walking stick knocked on the door. Again, he was the "interpreter of noises" for the family. I rose to meet him as the toddler led him through the hallway to the kitchen. He held a binder in his hand that read "Blind and Visually Handicapped." I was confused as this obviously blind man introduced himself and said we would be waiting for others to join us. I was now interpreting between the blind man with the big binder and the deaf couple who seemed as clueless as to what was about to transpire as I was. Finally, another knock at the door.

The young wife's family stood in the doorway. Her mother, father, and two siblings introduced themselves. They were all hearing. Some signed, while some used me to engage in conversation with the young couple.

The three-year-old was running from person to person, speaking with the hearing and using his advanced "baby signs" with the deaf.

After everyone had been seated in a semicircle around the small kitchen table, the man with the binder began the meeting. I sat directly across from the young wife. He began talking about the support his agency could give the family, particularly the young wife and mother. It soon became clear that she had recently been diagnosed with retinitis pigmentosa, a type of progressive vision loss. What also became clear was that this young mother had not been told to what extent her blindness would progress.

She lurched toward my chair and stood, her body shaking. With her hands speaking and my voice interpreting the words, she cried out, "I am deaf—I cannot be deaf *and* blind. I have a small child! I have a new baby! How will I care for them?" She looked desperately at her husband and then her family, with the slow realization that they had been told before her. *They were here to soften the blow.*

This was when I first learned about vicarious trauma. I was the secondary in the room—the language flowing to and fro, from my hands and my voice. It was one of the experiences as a freelancer that helped mold my business plan for my business for years to come. *Give the interpreter anything and everything we can to help them prepare for an assignment. NO surprises. No walking into a situation and being blindsided.*

There were many other instances of walking into situations without the appropriate information and trying to "maintain" and do my job. All of these helped me build the framework for what my agency would look like in the future.

CHAPTER 14

Working With the Famous and Infamous

Every freelance interpreter has stories about working with someone famous. This is called "platform interpreting" for a speaker or entertainer of some sort on a platform. Once you are an established interpreter and rise to the level of platform interpreting, you will sooner or later find yourself standing next to a person of stature or celebrity.

For me, there were several. The most memorable was Magic Johnson. I was several years into freelancing, and I received a call from Cornell University. Magic Johnson was coming to speak on campus, and they wanted to make it accessible to anyone deaf that wanted to attend. I announced that night at dinner that I was to interpret for Magic Johnson. My then 16-year-old son, Justin, stopped eating and stared at me as if he was trying to absorb my words. "Magic *Johnson*?" were the only words that came out. Justin was an avid basketball player and was on his school's Junior Varsity team. It had been a rough year for him. He had previously played under a coach who had put him in the games as a starter. The high school then replaced him with a coach whose son also played Justin's position. He ended up spending more time on the bench that season than on the court. He was hurt and disappointed but took it graciously. I knew taking him with me to see Magic Johnson speak would be something special.

Now I could not take my son on an assignment with me, but I could buy him a ticket and drop him off at the auditorium door. It happened that same night Justin had a basketball game at his high school. He explained to the coach that he was going to be leaving early to see Magic Johnson speak and I picked him up inside the school gym. As I walked in, one of the volunteers for the game handed me a program for the game which listed the starters from both schools and their stats. I stuffed it in my coat pocket, and we were off to Cornell.

Once I dropped Justin off out front of the building hosting the event, I found the green room and was introduced to Magic. He was incredibly gracious and offered to let me interpret on stage next to him to give better access to anyone deaf attending. We chatted about his talk, which was part of my prep, to gain a clearer understanding of what his topics would be and to start my brain thinking about what vocabulary might be used. As we talked, it became obvious that part of his talk would be about his family. He asked me if I had kids and I explained that I had just picked up my youngest to come hear him speak from his own high school basketball game. I also mentioned why this had been a rough season for Justin, because of the coaches changing, and so on. He told me his son was also 16 and he understood the challenges for kids that age, stating his son faced the challenge of other's unreasonable expectations because of who his father was. At one point he said, "Do you have anything to write on?" I pulled the only thing I had on me, out of my coat pocket: the Homer High School basketball game program for that night. He took it from me and wrote, "Justin—never give up, Magic." It is now framed and sits in my son's office 20 years later.

CHAPTER 15

Football and Interpreting

There were other famous people I met and interpreted for over the years: Jane Goodall, Hilary Clinton, Bill Cosby, and John McCain. Politicians and comedians. Authors and musicians. It was always an honor and always a pleasure. But the most fun I ever had interpreting was when I received the call that Marcus, an all-American athlete from Syracuse, was going to be attending SUNY Cortland and they were in need of an interpreter for his classes and all of his athletics. He was deaf, an amazing athlete—who was in *Sports Illustrated*—the "Who's Who" of upcoming athletes. As an all-American, he had three different sports to choose from: baseball, basketball, and football. He was highly recruited by many different colleges, but his mother wanted him close to home. So, he was coming to SUNY Cortland. And he chose football.

The next year with Marcus was the most fun I ever had interpreting and the most challenging. I knew nothing about football and was about to be interpreting all his team meetings, positional meetings, and practices, and I'd be on the sideline in the coach's box at every game. I literally picked up the equivalent of a "beginner's guide to football," which was meant for third and fourth graders, and then went to the closest deaf club to hang out with anyone who knew football and learn as much football vocabulary in sign that I could. In all the college classes and all my experience on assignments over the years, I had not picked up much in terms of football signs—only a few interpreting for high schoolers gym class. But now I needed to know more than "touchdown," "field goal," or "penalty." I now needed to be familiar with all aspects of the game and all the terminology.

Once being the wife and mother that moaned when football games were on TV, I was now the first one front and center, taking notes and asking my son and husband about everything I saw. "What does that flag mean? What are special teams? What? What? What?" They were great about answering all my questions and I was eating it up.

I loved working with Marcus—he was fun and *funny*. The team was also great and wanted to learn signs and hang out with him. A lot of that was Marcus himself. He had a natural charisma about him and a way that made everyone comfortable. And I was always there—in the classroom, at his meetings with his team, and going over videos of their games. I remember standing in the aisle of a team bus careening down the highway at 80mph. While I rocked back and forth, trying not to tumble over, the coaches were going over plays for the upcoming games on the bus, and I was there standing next to them in the aisle of the bus—sometimes for hours.

I was also on the field during practices, running back and forth from the sideline to the huddles. One time, the team was losing a game and during half time, one of the coaches grabbed me as they were about to go into the locker room. "They want you in there for Marcus," he demanded. Ok, well ... this was a place I had never been invited to, nor wanted to enter, but the coach was upset with the team and as I stood in the middle of these big, sweaty, dirty football players, my hands punching the air, emphasizing the emotion the coach was displaying, I realized suddenly that there was another outsider in this dark and stinky locker room. The associate pastor from my church had been invited to be the team chaplain, and he entered the room as this passionate lashing was coming out of the coach's mouth, laced with profanity, while simultaneously coming off my hands. A time when "staying in the moment" was definitely a challenge. But, it was my job and Marcus needed me. My hands kept flying ....

It honestly was the best assignment I had while freelancing. I loved learning something so different and working with such a funny and nice kid.

CHAPTER 16

What Makes a Good Interpreter?

During my tenure as a freelancer, I was always in high demand. Please know I was not the most skilled ASL interpreter out there, but I was always booked weeks in advance. Looking back now, as an agency that continually hires interpreters, I can see why I was so valued by agencies.

It helps to understand first that the profession of interpreting is not that old. The first interpreters were often found as volunteers, mostly from religious organizations such as churches or synagogues. Later, they came from disability services or some kind of other human service agency. These were well-intentioned, bilingual people who wanted to help others in whatever setting communication was needed. Sometimes it was casual, but often times formal and crucial settings such as education, medical, or even legal environments. It wasn't until the 1970s that interpreting became a recognized profession and the need for formal education was realized. It was about the same time that interpreter training programs were funded by the federal government and started slowly being offered across the country.

With so much focus on the deaf or limited English proficiency (LEP) persons and with the profession so new, often professional boundaries were lost or even discouraged. We were known as "helpers" or "volunteers," not as trained professionals, and for good reason. Often these first interpreters were acting as advocates or social workers—advising the people we served, giving them rides to appointments, and often care-taking more than interpreting. It put interpreters in the misunderstood role of "helpers" and not the professionals that they were.

When I started interpreting in 1993, I came from a pretty buttoned-up corporate environment in the automobile business. I knew the customers were the ones paying for my services. And I knew they needed to view me as a professional and differentiate my role from what was previously seen as a "helper." I wore a business suit, had business cards printed, and showed up early to each assignment. Very early. In the beginning, unsure of my skills, I put a *lot* of prep into each job. I came ready to work and with as much background knowledge as I could obtain.

I answered all calls and e-mails as soon as possible, always by the end of the day. My rates were reasonable, and I was always open to negotiation. Hence, my "dance card" was always full. That "dance card" later became the catalyst to my opening Empire Interpreting Service.

CHAPTER 17

A Laminated Card and My Love for My Dad

My dad. I loved, no, I *adored* my dad. I leaned into everything he had to say. You had to, because he was never loud or boastful. He was a kind, quiet man who always had a smile and a way about him that demanded respect without him ever asking for it. He never raised his voice or spanked us kids growing up. But, one "I'm really disappointed" would turn us into sniffling, crying little beings. It was because we never wanted to let him down. We wanted him to be proud of us and to do the right thing, like *he* always did.

In business, that meant the highest level of integrity and ethics, which is what I built my business on. Whenever I struggled with a decision that involves ethics or keeping high standards, I thought of my dad sitting next to me, and then I made my decision. My dad was the catalyst for

Figure 17.1 My dad and I

me seeing that there was a business brewing just under the surface of my career as a freelance interpreter.

Interpreters are employed through either being hired on as staff, freelancing through language service providers (businesses such as mine), or contracting directly with entities. For most of us starting out, we sign on with several language service providers and fill our schedules or a mixture of both agency work and direct to business work. That was my model.

Having come from the professional and conservative corporate workforce of the auto industry, I approached my work in that fashion. I took my career seriously and was constantly trying to improve my skills and relationships with the people paying for my services and the deaf community I was working with. I had a good reputation, a solid one, as someone very dependable and willing to take on almost any assignment if I was available. Consequently, my schedule was always full. And when a business would call with a request that I could not fill, I would give them the name and number of a colleague that I respected and was happy to pass on the work to. Those names were incredibly important to me and carefully chosen as I knew they would reflect my standards.

On one of those days, I was sitting next to my dad having coffee. My cell phone rang. My dad had his coffee mug to his lips and quickly motioned with his free hand, "go ahead, pick it up," and I did. It was a customer who had a request for dates I was already booked for. I pulled out a laminated card with the names and number of other interpreters I would entrust to pass on—interpreters I knew who had the same skills and ethics I had.

Once I ended the call, dad quizzically picked up the laminated card and asked me what had just transpired. I explained, I received these calls so many times during the week, I decided to make up a laminated card to keep in my Day-Timer (in the days before iPhones) for easy access to other interpreter names if I could not take on an assignment offered to me. My dad lightly tapped the laminated paper with my colleagues' names and said, "Terre, do you understand the value of this card? These places are calling you because they know and entrust you with the work. And you are giving it away."

The rest is predictable for you, the reader, but, at the time, I argued with my dad, thinking that how could I, a townie in rural central New

York with nothing but street smarts, become a business owner? My dad looked back and said nothing. I guess I had forgotten that he also had left school at 15 and had joined the Air Force and became a successful and well-respected person in our little town, degreeless and all. I was suddenly embarrassed by my self-deprecation.

The next year, my dad was diagnosed with a terminal illness, and he was gone quickly. In my grief for my dad and with my youngest then off to college, I was left alone in my sorrow with nothing but my father on my mind. It was in one of those moments I picked up that laminated card yet again and heard my father's words of encouragement to begin my own adventure as an entrepreneur. The next week, Empire Interpreting Service was born.

CHAPTER 18

Don't Be a Little Girl; Be a Businesswoman

There was another conversation I had had with my father regarding starting my own business that I feel needs to be told. As he pushed me to explore the entrepreneurial side of myself, I would push back with excuses:

"But Dad, I think people would HATE me if I told them their status quo wasn't good enough, would resent me when I refused to compromise, and probably would be downright angry at me if (stumbled on the words), if I became a competitor." His reply set me back in my chair: "Stop being a little girl about this!"

"Stop being a little girl?" That was Dad's advice? I was trying to process what he meant and totally ignored the last part of that sentence: "and start your own business." I so respected my dad and all I ever wanted was for him to be proud of me, and having him say I was acting like a "little girl" was a knife in the heart.

I pushed my coffee aside and met my Dad's eyes. "What do you mean 'a little girl'?"

Come on Dad! I was always the responsible one! I had my first (babysitting) job at 10 years old and worked full time from the age of 15. I was the one that people turned to when they needed the job done; I volunteered first, worked the hardest. Tried to make you proud. I worked through 12 months of chemotherapy and went to college simultaneously. Pushing through my bachelor's program in 18 months. Me?! A little girl? This needed some explaining.

"Little girls whine," he explained. "They look for ways to manipulate change in those around them while still keeping everyone happy and in harmony. It's just not the real world. At least, not the adult world. Businesswomen elicit change; they initiate momentum toward setting the bar higher; they bring forth a set of standards that elevate the profession. Start your own business. That is how you pioneer change."

He went on. "Little girls need to be patted on the head and told they are sweet, good, and loved. They look for constant approval and change who they are to make others like them. But they never change the world. You're not a little girl; your approval needs to come from within. You're a businesswoman and you can do this." And I did.

CHAPTER 19

The Loan Library at Barnes & Noble

Mourning my father's death and determined to start my own business, I looked to the one place I had always felt I could escape to. Books. Behind books, I could bury myself in learning and escape some of the pain I felt living without my dad in my life.

I sat at the furthest table from the baristas at the Barnes & Noble (B&N) Café counter. I surrounded myself with Peter Drucker, Henry Ford, and Jack Welch. My mini fort made of walls of business books hid the fact that I had been milking the same coffee for three, four, sometimes five hours. This was my "school of management," my "how to become an entrepreneur" class. Every night. And every Saturday and Sunday for months.

You see, once I had said out loud and put into the universe "I'm going to start my own business," I knew I would move forward. Once I had committed publicly, I was too proud and stubborn to not go through with it. What I didn't know was where I would glean the information needed to start a business from the ground up. Out of nothingness. Then, I found my college. Here, I received my business degree, from B&N.

I still frequent Barnes & Noble stores and I now buy books I'll never read. When I now go to the café, I order coffee, lunch, and dessert. I feel like I need to pay back my alma mater that gave me all that free business advice over 20 years ago.

CHAPTER 20

Ya-Ya Sisterhood at the Credit Union

A few months of sitting in bookstores while simultaneously grieving my dad was finally becoming too much self-absorption and not enough action. Determined to take the first step in starting my business, I sat at my desk in my home office, contemplating what I would need to do next.

I pulled myself up to a beautiful antique mission oak desk that my father had refinished. The desk made me feel close to my dad, sitting there, hands atop this desk, looking out the window of my home office. The ironies were all around me. I was starting an interpreting business in a town that had next to no diversity. I looked harder at my surroundings and saw more irony. Atop that beautiful antique desk, in sharp contrast, sat my bright blue iMac with its plastic bubble sides and plastic white corded mouse. How to move forward. *What else would I need?*

My mind again went back to my dad. An entrepreneur at heart and always forward thinking. He was the first to tell me about the "thing that would change the world," the Internet, and how I had to get a computer and get "hooked up," even when few of us knew what the Internet was. Thinking about that conversation and how he was proven right, I knew the first thing I wanted to spend money on was a website. After searching for a website designer, I knew I would need $3,500 to get it up and running. Back then, websites were not something the average person tackled. We all needed a designer. Along with the $3,500, I estimated $1,500 for a logo, business cards, and brochures.

With my business plan in hand and to ask for a meager $5,000, I entered our local community credit union. I loved doing business with them as they were completely about community and women led. Bob and I had gotten our car loans, mortgage, and credit cards from this credit union. We were long-time customers with great FICO scores and a familiarity of everyone from the tellers to the branch manager. I walked in, wanting to be independent from taking that $5,000 out of our family budget or putting it on a credit card that I shared with my husband. This business was my dream, my business-to-be, and I had 10 years of experience as a freelance interpreter, and therefore, the income to back up a small request of $5,000.

After approaching the teller, dressed in my best-looking black pant-suit and briefcase, I waited for her to hand me an application form. I saw her retreat into the manager's office instead. Thinking the manager would be excited to see my design for my newly formed business and to support another female professional, the words "Ya-Ya Sisterhood" popped into my head.

I was more than taken aback. I was completely deflated when she, quite smugly, explained they'd be happy to consider my request as soon as my husband came back with me to guarantee the loan.

Suffice it to say, I never darkened their door after that visit. I wish I knew who that female manager was today. I'd love to shove my financial statements at her and let her be the one to feel small 20 years later.

CHAPTER 21

Too Small for Their Business

Like many entrepreneurs, I started my new enterprise out of my house. I quickly transformed our home office into my headquarters, slowly integrating pieces from other rooms. I took possession of my husband's prized mission oak desk that my dad had given him upon completing his master's degree. It was placed as the focal point of the room adorned with my contemporary and cool blueberry Mac. And I was in business!

I spent hours and hours reading business books at the beginning of my entrepreneurial days. One of those books I read, *Word Perfect for Dummies*, instructed me on how to produce marketing materials, including printing my own brochures. My living room floor was routinely covered with envelopes that would be stuffed during my downtime in front of the TV. I used the Internet to compile a list of hundreds of potential customers and I sent information to them all, disgustingly licking too many envelopes and slapping on thousands of address labels until I had to walk away to give my aching back a break from all the sitting cross-legged and bending over.

The one piece of advice from all my business books I had read was to make sure you had professionally done business cards and not to print them on your own. I came up with a logo and looked for a printing company. Using my most "professional" voice, I called and made an appointment to talk about "an important order for my business." They assigned me a salesman who suggested we meet at a local restaurant for coffee.

I still smile when I think of that meeting at a Friendly's restaurant with the salesman from a local printing shop. He was a bit taken aback when he saw that I had just started my business. "We normally deal with established, bigger clients," he snarled, I'm sure assuming he'd just wasted his time. "Well, I normally don't conduct business in a Friendly's," I shot back, "And just for the record, my company will someday need thousands of business cards a year, so try and think to the future. I promise if you fill my order now, I will be loyal to your company as my company grows."

He told me my order wasn't big enough for him to deal with and quickly departed.

And when he came knocking on my door a few years later, I told him that our orders were probably too large for his small business.

CHAPTER 22

Meatloaf and Mashed Potatoes

Finally having my new logo and business cards in hand was great, along with my handmade brochures; however, finding places and people to give them to was another issue. My first invitation to positioning myself to talk about my new enterprise was the local Rotary Club. They had gotten my name from a mutual acquaintance regarding wanting information on interpreting and how interpreters could be utilized for some outreach into different communities.

During the conversation, they broached the idea of me coming to their next meeting and speaking on the subject. That one meatloaf and potatoes dinner in the back of the local Holiday Inn and my 15-minute spiel during dessert led to many more similar nights where I would spread the word about my new company and the benefit in utilizing our services. I became the guest speaker for months at every fire house, and civic, church, and volunteer group within the four counties of my home. And the word got out. Recognition of my business name grew, and calls were coming in.

It was working. The business grew. In six months, I had outgrown my home office with my little blueberry Mac and I was on the search for "real" office space and my first employee, who turned out to be my "mini-me," helped me grow my business from myself and six other interpreters to where we are today: myself, five employees, and more than 150 interpreters.

Who knew that meatloaf and mashed potatoes were so powerful?

CHAPTER 23

RFPs???

During the first two years of my business, I spent a lot of time still in the field, interpreting and filling jobs. One of the places I was called to often was a state office about an hour away. I had been told that the agency they had been using was only able to fill 40 percent of their requests, so they would call Empire Interpreting Service (EIS) and I would fill the requests left open. My contact there was a woman named Betty. Betty was acting as a staff interpreter and had been given the task to try to find outside interpreters when the contracting agency had no one. Betty had known me from years past when we would be teamed together for jobs in her area. We worked well together, and I always gleaned much from her. She was a CODA (Child of Deaf Adults) and had been interpreting basically her entire life. She had 20+ years of experience before I had ever learned to sign my ABCs, and I enjoyed her professionalism and love for the language.

After a year or so of helping fill in the gaps for this office, I informed Betty that I would be happy to send other interpreters from EIS; however, I had made the difficult decision to stay in the office and run the agency, as it had gotten to the point where I was needed for the day-to-day and if we were to grow, I felt I needed to be on site.

That same year, on Memorial Day weekend, I decided to go into the office to catch up some work late on Saturday morning. I was surprised to see Betty's number come up when the phone rang and turned from my paperwork and coffee to pick up the phone. "Terre, my boss wants to know if there's a reason why you haven't responded to the RFP for the work in our office?" was the first thing she said. Thank God, I was sitting at my computer so I could do a quick search on RFP, because I honestly had no idea what it was. "Request for proposal," Google responded. "Um, I had no idea there was an RFP out for your agency." Betty replied, "It's due on Monday and *my boss was hoping EIS was going to respond,*" she said, again bemoaning the fact that they were dealing with so many unfulfilled requests.

Another Google search and I found the RFP she was talking about. Completely unaware of what this undertaking would be, I told her I would personally drive it to the appropriate office on Tuesday morning, since that Monday was Memorial Day. That gave me what was left of Saturday, Sunday, and Monday to work on it. How hard could it be, right?

Two hours later, I was calling my husband to tell him I had this great opportunity to bid on a five-year contract with a state agency and needed to get an RFP in by Tuesday. *He knew what an RFP was*, and because of that, he responded with a sigh, "I'll see you Tuesday morning then," and he was right.

I quickly realized I would need to talk to my CPA, my attorney, and my insurance agent. And I would need coffee ... lots and lots of coffee. Three days later, I emerged from my office, exhausted and not so enthusiastic, but full of knowledge that I had absorbed through osmosis of that 87-page document. Knowledge I should have had. Things I should have known. Ugh, another street-smart school of learning.

I ran home, showered, and, back in my black business suit, meticulously put the RFP in triplicate into my briefcase and headed the hour-and-a-half drive away. There was exactly one Starbucks on the way and that would be the only stop between my office and handing over this precious document to the office of contracts for the state.

We were awarded the RFP. Over the next 15 years, we were awarded and rewarded the contract with this department. We eventually won additional contracts with them from New York City to Buffalo and everywhere in between. That one RFP was a catalyst for the company. There would be dozens of RFPs in our future and eventually, I would teach my department directors how to write their own. All started by a serendipitous phone call on a holiday weekend.

I think many small businesses don't grow because they just don't know. Today, we are on all of the state and national lists for RFP opportunities, and they are sent directly to our e-mails so that we may decipher which ones we would like to respond to. It was how we scaled our business, and it is how any small business can. Learn what you don't know.

CHAPTER 24

When the Competition Loses Their Cool

When I started Empire Interpreting Service, I had been a freelance interpreter for 10 years. I had worked directly with customers and through various language service providers (agencies) in the state. Wanting to be very ethical and above board, I let each agency know that I was starting my own business and that I had no intentions of going to customers that they had sent me to under their private contracts to try and undercut them. I would find new customers, in highly underserved areas, and only be of service to them. In retrospect, it was a very "little girl" thing to do.

It wasn't long before I realized how naive I was. As my business quickly grew, I was being approached by entities where I had worked as a freelance interpreter but that were now looking for new vendors and/or RFPs that were coming across my e-mail as new business opportunities. Some of these were places I had previously done an assignment at one time or another in my decade freelancing through another agency. I quickly realized my original promise could not be a forever one or I would never scale my business.

One such RFP was a statewide contract to provide services to a very large area of the state and was awarded to my company during our third year in existence. One male competitor had been awarded this state contract for decades before I opened my business. He was obviously not happy when he found out it was not automatically reawarded to him. He knew me because I had done some work for him in another part of the state. And he reached out to make sure and let me know he was *not happy*.

I had just driven for eight hours to attend a regional conference for interpreters. As I was checking into my hotel room, loaded with bags, my briefcase, and my purse, and trying to pull out my plastic room key, my cell phone rang. I dropped everything (as all business owners know, we respond 24/7 when called) and answered my phone. A very deep, angry, and loud voice shouted "Terre. Terre Slater?" to which I responded, "Yes, can I help you?" not knowing what or who was on the other line. "This is Sam from ABC Interpreting!!!" He continued on very slowly and emphatically, emphasizing each word.

"I-don't-know-who-you-think-you-are-*little girl,* but we are going to have a sit-down and you are going to explain to me what you *think* your plans are for your business. You won't be taking business away from me!"

"Little girl?!" Was he joking?! I picked up my cell phone and slammed it repeatedly on the closest table, then, picking it up quickly, I said, "I think we must have a really bad connection because *I know* you didn't say what I *think* you just said." And I hung up. I serviced that state contract for the next 15 years until I eventually turned it down because I felt the terms were not beneficial to my company or my interpreters anymore. Little did he know how he spurned me on over the last two decades with his "little girl" comment.

Revenge is not a dish that you serve cold. True revenge is quiet success.

CHAPTER 25

Bootstrapping

It honestly never occurred to me to have a marketing budget when I started my business. Social media platforms weren't popular yet and people weren't advertising on them. I was trying to get the word out by volunteering to be a speaker at any community groups I could get an invitation to and by attending any networking events I could find.

I handed out business cards and brochures like crazy but wasn't getting my name into the hands of my target markets: medical facilities and educational institutions.

When I was freelancing, I would always carry business cards that I had made; the agencies I worked through did not provide them. And when I entered a medical facility, it was the receptionist that I gave my card to. They were the one that had called for an interpreter and were the person that would most likely be calling in the future. I knew that this was the person I needed to get my business name in front of.

So I went back to the floor of my living room. I stuffed 8×11 manila envelopes with my brochures, business cards, and a laminated card with adhesive strips on the back. The front of that card had our name, our 24/7 number, and our logo. The receptionist, whether in an emergency room or the front office of a doctor's office, could stick that card to any surface and have our number in front of them. They wanted their problem solved: how to communicate with someone present that could not speak their language. We would be the answer.

I then developed a list of all the hospitals and medical facilities I could find online and started lists. Pages and pages of lists. I meticulously put these packets together with logo stickers on the outside and the names of their facilities neatly typed across the front. As I folded the clasp on each one and put it onto a pile, I wondered how much money I had spent on these dozens of packets. This was marketing costs. Not something I was familiar or comfortable with. But I was about to have a huge payoff.

I recruited my youngest son, Justin. He put on his best and only business suit, jumped in his beloved Jeep that got him through college, and crisscrossed New York State. My only instruction: walk into the emergency room or front office and look for the receptionist. Hand *them* the packet and say only, "I was asked to drop this off to you," and leave.

And it happened. Our phones started ringing. Some scheduled appointments, some emergency room visits at 2 a.m. And we filled all the requests from our roster and when no one could go, I went! Some would say I was crazy; I had no contract with these places! They came after the fact. But I got my foot in the door in an unconventional way, and once they saw that we would produce and that we had professionals that could supply effective communication, we were on our way.

You don't have to have a marketing budget to get customers. Sometimes, street-smarts work. Sometimes, it's just old-fashioned door knocking.

CHAPTER 26

Ask the Entrepreneur

Opportunities often come from unforeseen places. A few years into my business, I was approached to co-write a local newspaper column, "Ask the Entrepreneur," with two other female business owners, each in various stages of our business. Questions would be posed about running a business and the three of us would each give a short answer, thereby giving the audience three varying perspectives.

It was time-consuming. We worked on a deadline and often we had no idea how the other two would respond. That meant not giving a knee-jerk reaction. It meant a thoughtful and well-researched response, which was then put it into one short paragraph. However, the name recognition was priceless. When I was introduced to someone, often the response back would be "You're the 'Ask the Entrepreneur' contributor!" It also allowed me to connect with other entrepreneurs and lend credibility to who I was as a business owner. Again, the return on investment (ROI) factor. Much like the constant public-speaking opportunities, name recognition is priceless. Don't shy away from those opportunities, as the payback *will* be there.

I admit, looking back at some of my answers sent to "Ask the Entrepreneur" makes me cringe, as today I would answer much differently. However, I did find a pretty timely entry that gives an example of questions and answers.

"Ask the Entrepreneur" from 24 August 2010:

Question from reader:

"I'm going into my first Fall season with my new business. Do you have any suggestions for things I should be focusing on?"

Theresa:

Fall is a great time to "put your house in order" for the upcoming year. First, you should meet with your CPA to go over your financial statements and know your position regarding tax liabilities. Don't wait until late in the year or early next year to find out you need to scrape together a large sum of money to pay taxes in April.

Then, plan to meet with your insurance agent to go over policies. Do you have adequate insurances? Has your staff grown? Your inventory? Have you purchased new properties, or have they increased in value and need additional protection?

Third, look at your electronic records. Is each computer backing up on and offsite to protect your information? Do you have the encryption needed to protect proprietary information? This is an often-overlooked area of business and one that needs to be addressed yearly.

Addressing these three areas will give you a jump start into the next year!

CHAPTER 27

Language Wheel and Consumer Cards

Whenever I introduced myself and said, "I own an interpreting and translation company," I was most often asked, "How many languages do you speak?" This really used to annoy me, because did they think I personally was interpreting all the requests that came in? However, I realized soon that what they really wanted to know was "How many languages do you offer?"

This was especially important to one of our target markets: medical facilities. I would often hear stories from medical facilities of a person that needed an interpreter coming into an emergency room or doctor's office and not being able to communicate or even tell them what language interpreter they needed. After some brainstorming, the staff came up with the idea of a "language wheel."

The language wheel was basically a laminated piece of paper cut into strips and held together with a metal binder ring. On one side of each strip, it said in English, "I do not speak English and am in need of an interpreter," and on the flip side, it would say in each language we provide, for example, Spanish, "I do not speak English and am in need of an interpreter."

Language wheels were one of the little strokes of genius my staff came up with. Another one was empowering our consumers, people whose first language is not English, by making business cards for them. We coined them "Consumer Cards." We had staff business cards, and we went further by making up interpreter cards with their name, the languages they provided, and our contact information. One of my staff members came up with the idea of making cards that consumers could present when at the emergency room or doctor's office, or any time they might need an interpreter. They simply said the language that they needed and that they were requesting an interpreter. And, of course, our contact information was on the cards as well.

Find ways to get your name out there. Unconventional ways. Ways your competition hasn't thought of or is not doing. Bootstrap your business.

CHAPTER 28

What Is an LSP?

My business, in our industry, is known as an LSP: a language service provider. It just means that on some level, we are providing a service involving a language. For us, that began as providing onsite American Sign Language interpreters. As we grew, we added spoken language interpreters on site, and eventually we added translation services.

Today, we offer both sign language and spoken languages on site and virtually, and spoken languages over the phone. We also have a translation component that translates everything from legal documents to entire websites. In 2023, we added "on demand" interpreters virtually. This allows customers to sign into our app, request a language, and have an interpreter at their disposal in 90 seconds or less. And yes, technology and AI have greatly impacted the delivery of services.

We offer over 300 different languages, and, although that sounds so impressive, keep in mind there are currently over 6,000 languages in the world. You may be surprised that the top languages spoken in the world are English, Mandarin Chinese, Hindi, and then Spanish.

Top 10 languages, where they are the official language, and the number of speakers:

- **English:** 67 countries; 1.452 billion speakers.
- **Mandarin Chinese:** China, Taiwan, Singapore; 1.118 billion speakers.
- **Hindi:** India; 602 million speakers.
- **Spanish:** 21 countries; 534 million speakers.
- **Arabic:** 25 countries; 372 million speakers.
- **French:** 29 countries; 300 million speakers.
- **Bengali:** Bangladesh and India; 265 million speakers.
- **Russian:** Russia, Belarus, Kazakhstan, Kyrgyzstan; 258 million speakers.

- **Portuguese:** 10 countries; 223 million speakers.
- **Indonesian:** Indonesia; 200 million speakers.

Lingua Language Center, Broward College

Our industry has been deemed "the Biggest Industry You've Never Heard of" by United Language Group, an LSP that provides services worldwide with offices in seven countries. At the time of this declaration, they were predicting in 2020 that the industry would be a market of $45B. In 2022, the industry had an estimated value of $67B, and the prediction is now $98B by 2028.

The top five companies are between $575M and $1,160M. However, 31 percent of LSPs' total revenue is under $100K and 23 percent of LSPs have revenues of $10M+ and are made up worldwide of only 169 companies. The medium-sized LSPs are earning $100K to $10M annually. My company falls in the median of that range. I believe that has to do with our quick growth at the beginning of the business and the fact that I put on the brakes somewhere around year 15.

CHAPTER 29

The Cost of Ethics

Over my Sunday morning coffee and newspaper routine, I read an article entitled "How a Project Went Wrong." It was stunning and difficult to comprehend. Contractors had worked in a local high school removing asbestos without following safety protocol, contaminating the environment, and sending poisonous toxins into the air. I thought of the children and teachers going through their day, innocently breathing in and out.

But what was even worse? This happened *repeatedly*.

Shocking violations from vendors who had previously been cited for creating dangerous environments by ignoring industry protocols. Yet, these same businesses were awarded additional contracts in the same school district. Horrified as I again thought of these children breathing in killer chemicals, I dug further to find out **why**, and there it was *because they were the lowest bidder.*

At the beginning, my business was just an idea of "how to do it better." I had encountered far too many bilingual individuals acting as interpreters or translators with no formal training or certification, along with too many agencies I worked for that had no vetting process or support those of us in the field.

It was then that I decided to transform the experience for those utilizing interpreting services, along with realizing my vision of creating a more supportive and professional environment for the interpreters themselves. My "win–win" scenario was now my business plan.

But, I also found quickly that my plan came with a cost. With so many contracts dependent on only that bottom-line lowest bidder, it became our responsibility to prove that having higher standards means lower customer costs in the long run.

To our customers, it means different outcomes depending on the environment:

Medical environments: Doctor–patient communication is so critical. It assures medical professionals that their interpreters are familiar with medical terminology and understand the various medical environments. This allows for quicker diagnosis and treatments and less repeat visits, resulting in a healthier patient and a healthier doctor–patient relationship. Interpreters understand and abide by HIPAA and have professional liability insurance.

Business: There is a world of new markets available if language and cultural barriers are removed. Having accurate translations can open a floodgate of new opportunities, beginning with websites and social media and ending in business negotiations. With only one chance to make a first impression on the world, that first impression must be impeccable.

Education: Thousands of deaf and hard-of-hearing students utilize interpreters from elementary school to postsecondary settings. Having a highly skilled interpreter familiar with class content offers the best chance of success for students, alleviating repeating classes due to communication breakdowns and ensuring happier and more successful students.

The point is, when you have highly skilled, professional interpreters and translators that consider cultural and linguistic nuances, coupled with an agency experienced in making the correct matches, it is a win–win. Even when the "bottom-line" cost may initially seem higher. **You don't have to be the lowest bidder, you have to show you have the highest value.**

CHAPTER 30

The Magazine Cover

When the business was gaining success in upstate New York, I was asked to be on the cover of a local business magazine that was targeted at women. This was one of those moments that I knew being a presentable representation of my business was important. I had previously been featured in a magazine as one of three women talking about their business. Each was interviewed; each had a photo taken to go alongside their article.

When the photographer showed up at my office to take my photo, he was intrigued by the large windows overlooking the square below. "Beautiful lighting," he said. "Let's try something different." He insisted I not sit at my desk, but on the floor with a book, as if I had plopped myself down there and decided to work from the middle of my office. I knew enough about photography to know that the light streaming in from above would cast dark, sharp shadows across my face. And they did. The result was awful. I looked like an old lady curled up on the floor with black lines across her face. I looked for that photo so I could show you here on this page, but I could not find it anywhere. I'm sure I deleted all evidence of that photo shoot.

Unfortunately, at the time of the publication, a lot of people saw that awful picture. Everyone was polite. A few said, "nice article" and no one mentioned the picture. Until I walked into the next WPO (Women's Presidents Organization; more on them later) meeting. Well, the moderator of the group, who I considered the Grande Dame, had the article in her hand when I entered the enormous meeting room with the oversized conference table situated squarely under the light of the ostentatious chandelier.

She tapped the picture and said, "Terre, why in the world did you let this photo be published?" Well, to be honest, I had no idea I had a choice. And that's exactly what I said. She spent the next few minutes explaining to me that as the business had more exposure, there would

Figure 30.1 Photo by Cindy Bell, courtesy of Syracuse Woman Magazine

be more articles, more photographs, another reason to keep yourself polished, and more photographers to deal with. She told me that I should ask for veto power over any photos and refuse to take any pictures that would make me look silly or reflect badly on my business. I walked away feeling empowered and ready for the next time!

And, that time came. I had another opportunity for great exposure when the local women's business magazine asked me to be on the cover. I had learned by now that I needed to get help with my wardrobe, as several shots were to be used, and to have my hair and makeup done professionally. However, for the cover shot, the editor, via a cell call, was insisting that I be shot on the rooftop deck of our building with the expanse of the city in the background.

I objected strongly, and so did the photographer. She knew this would not be a good shot. No opportunity for fill light and on a very windy rooftop. The editor would not be deterred, and I felt the article may be pulled if I didn't comply. The photo wasn't terrible, but it wasn't great. My well-coifed hair was blown back, my eyes squinting into the wind and sun. I did feel it was worth the compromise to showcase my business and it was nowhere near as hideous as the photo on the floor.

However, know that you do have a choice when you have an opportunity to have your business promoted. I always grab those opportunities and often it's to speak at a business event or sometimes to community organizations. There will always be photos snapped and posted online, and no one expects those to be picture perfect. However, if you are being photographed for a publication, you should at least ask to see the photos before they are published. It might not always fly, as I found out with the magazine cover, but I have had many situations since then where the photographer was happy to let me edit photos as the shoot was happening.

CHAPTER 31

Publicity Begets Publicity

I have been told I'd sell my soul for the opportunity to talk about my company. One thing I do know is that publicity begets publicity. As I was running around the four corners of New York State, I was proving that theory and growing my business. I began looking for any opportunity to talk about my company or my industry. I contacted community groups, schools, and any other organization that would have me. Once I was on that circuit, many other offers came in to speak.

None of these were paid gigs. What they were was an opportunity for me to get the word out about my business and promote who we were and what we were doing. And it paid off big. There are so many groups in your industry where you can volunteer to speak. There are groups that might not be exactly in your industry but could be connected in some way to part of your target market. And there are always community organizations looking for their next speaker.

It does take a lot of work preparing. Putting together presentations is time-consuming. Taking time away from your office is also costly and puts a strain on your schedule. Some people would say they'd rather eat dirt and die than stand in front of people. I get that. Luckily for me, I overcame that fear during the time I was interpreting. I was always in front of someone, whether it be two individuals that needed me to bridge communication or an auditorium full of people. But, remember that you are speaking on a subject that no one knows better than you. And even if they know your industry, they don't know your business. *Speak from the heart and show your true passion for what you do.*

Be honest. Tell stories. Be totally transparent even when you're terrified. Again, be honest! The reason I am even writing this book is because of a presentation I gave at the Union League in Philadelphia at a BLF (Business Leadership Forum) breakfast. I was terrified to tell the true story of my rise to success. I was surrounded by doctors, lawyers, and Wharton

Figure 31.1 Theresa addresses a group of professional women to offer guidelines on operating a successful business

MBAs. *Who was I?* A kid out on her own at 15 with no education—who, although formally educated later in life, started out by just hanging on to survive one week to the next.

While my audience was graduating from high school, I was having a baby and working minimum-wage jobs. While they were in Ivy League universities, I was working as a waitress and cleaning hotel rooms. These successful members of this prestigious club were well spoken, well traveled, and, by any measure, successful people. It was terrifying standing in front of them.

I started out by telling them I was different. That I could not relate to their experiences except that I was now a successful businesswoman. I told my story honestly and thought, "What do I have to lose?" I had an audience to talk to about my business, and that was important. I could not have been more surprised by the enormous support from the people in the room. They were fascinated *because* my story was different. They asked questions. They shook my hand afterward and they were warm and receptive.

It was because of that talk that I was approached by a book editor and asked if I would consider writing a book about myself and how I built my company. Opportunities are everywhere and can so often be missed by not putting yourself front and center. Women especially feel that speaking about themselves and their successes can be viewed as crass or arrogant. And they worry about what others will think. Men are much better at this and often snatch up those opportunities while we're still sitting in the corner worried if we are worthy.

CHAPTER 32

Horizontal Business Model

Earlier, I alluded to learning the "horizontal business model" while waitressing at 15. What I was learning was that it is indispensable to a business that there always be more than one person who knows how to function in a single position. In the restaurant, I learned to be the backup for every position. In my willingness to please and worry I would lose my job (God forbid they find out I was only 15), I had stepped in and learned how to do everything from being the hostess to washing the dishes.

At Empire Interpreting Service, we still run the business in the same way. With a small support staff that runs the agency, we can each do the other's job. All of us can take a customer call, book an assignment, or be a support to the interpreters on site. There is no real hierarchy. I still answer the phone if everyone else is busy. I can jump in if any of the staff is out and conversely, they can jump in for most of my duties.

That is not to say that I'm not the one making executive decisions, meeting with our CPA, attorney, responding to RFPs, and so on. But, for the day-to-day, we can cover the other's back. This is especially crucial when running a small business. Being transparent and giving your staff autonomy is not what makes you a weak leader. Being a control freak and pigeonholing people into specific roles will make for a weak business.

As a 15-year-old waitress, I learned to step in for the hostess, dishwasher, and short-order cooks. I later learned how to do the cash out at the end of a shift, split tips, and write shift sheets for the manager. I was learning how to be indispensable. I was learning what a horizontal business model was in real time.

CHAPTER 33

The Responsibility of What You Do and My "Aha!" Moment

I've pointed out the chances you take in owning a business and the vision you have, the differences you want to make, and so on. But the bottom line is you shoulder a lot of responsibility. I didn't realize how much until an April night in Armory Square when we came together to celebrate the five-year anniversary of my business. Armory Square is a hub of entertainment, shopping, and nightlife in the middle of downtown Syracuse. Once a busy industrial area, it is now a cool and popular destination. I thought this was the best of the best for our get-together. The weight of that responsibility and the following Aha! moment came to me in the midst of our celebration.

I chose a place called The Ohm, an open environment with lots of room for mingling, inside and out. It was a very cool venue in the heart of Armory and surrounded by the energy of the city. And it had the space needed to accommodate our theme. We wanted the motif to reflect multiculturalism and decided to carry that through our variety of music, food, and art. We tapped into the talent of our interpreters: blues music and salsa dancing, stunning photographs depicting the people of Cambodia, the Lost Boys of Sudan's sculptures, and beautiful handmade jewelry from Ukraine. Every room was filled with different artisans' work, different culture's music, and food from different parts of the world.

It was so great! We were together in a place that made up the many facets of the languages and cultures that we had been born into or studied. We ate it, we saw it, our bodies felt it through the music, and we heard it in the different languages being spoken. I appreciated it, and for a short moment relaxed in it, relished it, and lived it!

And then I stood up to speak on an elevated platform—in the middle of the moment to thank everyone for their part in our success. As I looked up from my notes, it struck me mid-sentence that every one of these people, the interpreters, their significant others, my staff, and even my children and husband, all depended on the success of what I live every day. My business was how they paid their mortgage, bought groceries, and put gas in their car.

That was my Aha! moment: the vision and "coolness" of what we were doing was one thing, but the true gravity of it all and what it meant for the lives of every person in that room, that was something entirely different. The responsibility I felt in that moment is the blessing and the curse of every small business owner. It is a reminder of how what we do and how we do it impacts people's lives. Awesome? Yes. But it also creates a burden that is often impossible to carry.

CHAPTER 34

Overwhelmed

Amid a crazy busy workday in 2013, my iMac suddenly announced that it was "OVERWHELMED!"

I've had my car e-mail me that it needs an oil change and my Apple watch tell me to "get going" when I am behind on closing my activity circles. But never have I had my computer announce *it* is "overwhelmed."

It broke my train of thought *amid* my whirlwind day. I announced to my staff, "It's been such a busy day that even my Mac is overwhelmed. Time for a break!" I grabbed my ongoing Starbucks and started my Google search for "What does it mean when your computer says it's overwhelmed?" My results indicated that my computer's memory is getting full, and my backup wasn't going to be backing up if I didn't "dump" unnecessary files. Hence, my search began for movies, photos, and any big files that I could safely do without.

This really wasn't a day I could afford to be stopped in my tracks to try and sift through 10 years of business and personal files. Having no choice but to plow through hundreds of thousands of bits of information, I felt like a quality control person in a vegetable market throwing out the rotten and ugly, trashing the ones I no longer found palatable, and disposing of anything I thought I would never want to see again in the future.

What I was finding, in between the trash, were all the reasons that I own this business and push through the overwhelming days. There were pictures of the first building my then-husband and I purchased together for our businesses and our pride at being able to provide such a beautiful environment for staff.

There was picture after picture of me with Stacey, my first hire, who is still my confidante and friend and helps run my business. Then came the images of me with my two sons, Trevor and Jay, an unexpected benefit of the business, both coming on to work with me and the unimaginable blessing of being able to have that connection with them every day.

There were interpreters and staff, consumers, and celebrations! A second location in Syracuse, a third in New York City, a five-year anniversary with everyone there to relish the landmark year.

There were also sobering reminders. Pictures of a family friend put together for a tribute when he died so young. The vast amount of voice memos and pictures I had taken of my mom while she was in her last years, dying from dementia. A reminder that back then I pushed the business hard to move forward in order to fund her care. Images of business and real life intermixed with no boundaries.

Overwhelming? No, validating. What I spent the last 10 years building is a good thing, the *right* move for myself, my family, my industry, my interpreters, my consumers, and my customers.

Then, back to work. Both my iMac and I are feeling less overwhelmed and a little more "cleansed."

CHAPTER 35

Statistics on Women-Owned Businesses

Source: https://ecommercetips.org/women-in-business/

If I had ever looked at the statistics of starting a business and especially for women-owned businesses, I am sure I would never have taken the leap. However, looking back over 20 years as a business owner, I think we have reached encouraging milestones and yet sobering ones that we as a group need to take stock of remain. Some of those that resonate or shock me the most are:

- Ninety-nine percent of businesses across the United States are small businesses.
- Forty-two percent of all businesses in the United States are women owned.
- Failure rate:
  - Year 1—20 percent of businesses fail.
  - Year 2—30 percent of businesses fail.
  - Year 3—50 percent of businesses fail.

What are the reasons for these failures? Here are the two biggest that you need to pay attention to:

1. **Lack of market demand.** You may have a wonderful solution to a problem you face. You've seen those pitches on Shark Tank when Mr. Wonderful says, "You need to take this idea out back and shoot it." Do your due diligence. Know that what you're selling, whether a widget or a service, has a market demand.

2. **Running out of capital.** If your business is ever to grow at all, even a business like mine that began with a $5,000 American Express loan, there WILL come a time when you will need business capital. You will need a LOC (line of credit) and a relationship with a financial institution that not only understands you but understands your industry. An example of this follows about how to create and foster that relationship in my Key Bank story.

Know the statistics and the reasons for them. They don't dictate your future, but they help shape it. When you beat the odds, celebrate, and know you did something pretty amazing.

CHAPTER 36

Don't Go It Alone

When I started my business, I found myself in a strange sort of isolation. During my tenure as a freelance interpreter, I had a lot of camaraderie. There were regional and national groups to support interpreters. There were publications and books written where, within those pages, I could relate.

Now as a business owner and entrepreneur, living in a small upstate New York town, I knew no other female business owners. Locally, I had presented at the Rotary, Kiwanis, and Lion Clubs; however, rarely was there a woman in the audience. So, I started looking on the Internet for those business groups that represented women.

The first local group I found was an organization started by a woman in Syracuse, New York, called "Woman Ties." This group was formed to promote and foster relationships with other female business owners. It was a great first step for me. I met other women struggling with the same issues. I will always be grateful for that group and the inspirational founder. She ferociously supported my endeavors and helped open doors for marketing opportunities. However, there was a moment where I realized I had to push myself out of the comfort zone I'd developed with these ladies.

It was the fourth year of my business, and I was about to hit $1M in sales. The founder of Woman Ties had asked me to speak at a luncheon to encourage the women in the group. It was entitled "March to Millions" and a very big deal for me. From that laminated card with the six names of my fellow interpreters to a business that employed several office staff and over 100 interpreters, I was feeling very proud. And I wanted to share that with my sons and my husband, all of whom were extremely supportive of my dream.

I walked into the luncheon with my husband and one of my sons (the other lived too far away to attend) and was greeted with a frantic, "*This is for women only*," by a young woman taking names at the front door. When I explained that they were my husband and son, who was also my employee, she reluctantly led us to a round table set with fine china at the front of the room. And then, right as I was being introduced to speak, came a nervous whisper in my ear: "*They're going to leave after your talk, aren't they?*" This young volunteer took the idea that this was a group of women, by women, and for women *very* seriously. Although I understand she was missing the big picture, I saw that the pendulum had swung from only standing in front of men, to now only standing in front of women. It was also clear that, as much as I loved this group, I needed to expand my circle and not stay in a comfort zone where I was the largest business in the room. I needed to push myself forward. And then, serendipitously, I did.

Somehow the word was out there that I had made this presentation on my "march to millions" and I was contacted by the moderator of the Upstate New York Women Presidents Organization and invited to a meeting. Accepting that invitation opened doors I had not yet even thought of.

CHAPTER 37

Powerhouse Women and Their Support

The WPO

According to their website, the Women Presidents Organization (WPO) is a premier membership organization for women leaders of privately held, multimillion-dollar companies. To quality for membership, candidates must run the day-to-day of their company and have an ownership interest, and the company must have gross annual sales of $2M for a product-based company or $1M for a service-based business.

To say I was floored with an invitation to join this group would be an understatement. I initially wasn't even sure how they knew about me. However, the phone call came and an invitation to attend a meeting was extended. I enthusiastically accepted! I had met dozens of women entrepreneurs, so I felt comfortable finding out what this group was all about However, this group of women was definitely next level.

I walked into the boardroom on the third floor of a 200-year-old office building in downtown Syracuse and suddenly felt very small. The boardroom was inside the building that housed Key Bank, one of the sponsors of the WPO and their monthly meeting place. The meeting was after banking hours, so I was directed to a side door where a well-dressed security guard ushered me up the back marble stairs. The stairs led to an extremely large, extremely old, and ornate conference table with a chandelier hanging ostentatiously above. Inside that very large boardroom, I felt small, *really small,* and suddenly incredibly nervous.

As I looked around the room, I saw several very well-dressed, successful women. Outfits that were meticulously put together. Jewelry, briefcases, and shoes to match. I again felt very small. My $1M in sales suddenly felt like less of a success. I realized quickly that I was starting from the bottom with this group.

I was immediately greeted warmly by the moderator and led to a seat. There were beverages and dinner that would be served during a later break in the meeting. She explained the meeting would be three hours. "*What would we talk about for three hours?*" I thought to myself. Later, I realized we could have stretched the meeting to six hours and still had things to talk about.

At the beginning of the meeting, each woman introduced herself and talked about her business. There were interjections here and there of issues attendees were facing: Accounts Receivable (AR), employment problems, looking for a new CPA, negotiating contracts. The list went on. I felt more and more like someone was finally speaking my language and that I might, just might, belong to this group.

CHAPTER 38

Key Bank

The women from the WPO became my unofficial Board of Advisors. It was here I could safely talk about issues I faced as a female business owner. It was here I was given advice and had my feet held to the fire to improve and grow my business. It was also here that the WPO most likely saved my business. As I felt more comfortable with the group and realized that I was in a safe place to talk about the challenges of running my business, I knew I could bring issues to the table and receive thoughtful, helpful advice.

During the loan crisis in 2008, many banks were re-evaluating and reorganizing their customer base. For my business, this meant that the small credit union I had my business accounts with, including my line of credit (LOC), was calling in loans. And no, this was not the credit union I spoke about earlier in the book. This one was out of town.

We had never carried debt on the business; however, we did need an LOC to pay interpreters and staff regularly while we waited for large payments on contracts that often came in months after the work was completed. The credit union we were using for the business had decided in the crisis of 2008 to close all business accounts and call in any small business loans and LOCs.

At that time, I owed approximately $60K on my line of credit. I *did not have* $60,000 sitting in my business bank account, or obviously I wouldn't have dipped into the LOC, and I was panicked. This was not a climate where other financial institutions were going to take a chance on a five-year-old business who couldn't even pay off their LOC.

I walked into the next WPO meeting feeling for the first time since opening EIS that I might be closing. I felt vulnerable and stupid for putting my business in this position and I needed to come clean with the group. The response I received was not what I expected. First, they were shocked I had bootstrapped the business and wasn't in debt outside the

LOC. Second, the moderator stood up and said, "Done!" and gave me a business card with the President's name of Key Bank, Central New York. "I'll make an introduction," she announced, and then went on to the next topic as if this was put to bed. Done and done!

Four days later, Stephen Fournier, the Key Bank district president, walked into my conference room. Professional and polished, he was also warm and understanding. An hour later, he walked out, and we had transferred our accounts to Key Bank, who he explained was very invested in helping women-owned businesses succeed. As he walked away, I looked at my CFO in disbelief. We had a new bank. We had a new support system. And we had a $350K LOC. I doubt Mr. Fournier knew he had saved my business that day, but I will never forget that meeting and the trust he invested into my company.

My CFO quickly cut a check for the $60K owed on the credit union's LOC. I drove the 30 minutes to their location in nearby Ithaca and personally thanked my point of contact there for their service during our first five years in business and ceremoniously held out the check and closed accounts as if I never had a second thought about them calling in our loan and pulling the rug out from under us. I had landed on my feet! Key Bank has since been there for my business and me personally, through business loans, auto loans, and mortgages—and through COVID. They are truly a bank for women entrepreneurs.

CHAPTER 39

Outgrowing Your Experts

Although the banking crisis in 2008 forced my hand in terms of moving from the credit union to Key Bank, I had truly outgrown what a credit union could offer. I quickly found one of my other "Four Corners" of outside consultants also needed to be replaced.

What I call my "Four Corners" are my CPA, banker, attorney, and insurance broker. I will talk more about the necessity of each later in the book. For now, I want to talk about outgrowing my CPA and what that looked like.

Everyone looks for a CPA when they begin their business and for me, it was easy. I had a past connection to a CPA that I had worked with when I was a bookkeeper in a former job. He had been a great support system to me at the time I was moving from receptionist to bookkeeper in that business. I thought because he helped teach me how to create financial statements, he would be a person I felt connected to and comfortable with. I never asked for references. I never thought to research what size businesses he worked with or even what his costs would be. I only thought I needed a CPA and knew this person. And poof! He was my accountant.

For the first few years of working with this CPA, I felt like that frightened receptionist again, learning from the highly educated and all-knowing accountant who had to "mansplain" everything to me. The truth of the matter was that he was teaching me how to take numbers and plug them into line items on a financial statement. He never taught me what a financial statement could tell me or how to read it. And honestly, that wasn't his job.

So now, flash forward 15 years, I was again feeling like that uneducated receptionist sitting at the feet of the learned CPA and only needing to give him the numbers he needed to plug into his programs and spit out tax returns. For the first few years, that is.

As the years went on and I had hired a bookkeeper, I felt further away from my numbers and honestly was not paying close attention as my business was growing so fast. When I did have that end of the year meeting with my CPA, I still felt like the student and he, the teacher. I felt clueless, small, and like I did not understand my numbers.

In 2008, when I had the jolt from the Credit Union and moved to Key Bank, I had to confront the fact that I needed to dig more deeply into our numbers and really understand what financials I needed and how they related to the health of my business. I also needed someone that was not so intimidating that I dare not ask questions.

One of the members of the WPO was a partner at a large accounting firm. She was smart and savvy and talked about financials, tax implications, profit margins, and cost of sales in a way that I could understand. She didn't make me feel small or ignorant. I finally felt like I could ask questions. The more I dug into my financials and really started to have a clearer understanding, the more I found I was losing money on many fronts. One of those was a mistake that had been made on a tax return. Whether it was numbers given to the CPA that were erroneous or whether he had made the mistake was unclear. What was clear is that by me being a good little student and not speaking up, I was losing part of my hard-earned money.

So, I started asking questions. I felt empowered by what I had learned and went back to my corner at Barnes & Noble, reading everything I could on financials for small businesses and what I should be looking for. I asked for quarterly meetings and not just an end of the year exchange of numbers and then signing off on a tax return I really didn't understand. I felt an uneasy pushback as our roles slowly reversed. I asked why I was paying what I was paying and exactly how his time was calculated. By the end of that year, I knew I needed to make a change.

I truly liked this CPA. He was someone I would have chosen to be a friend if we had met under other circumstances. I felt I owed him something as he helped me move up in a business so many years ago. I realized that I was "being a little girl" about it, so I decided to be a businesswoman. I set up a time to meet at a local restaurant. I asked for a table that was well lit and big enough to look over documents. I showed up early and sipped my coffee, getting my nerve up to let him know I was moving on.

He showed up late carrying a large tax organizer with *Empire Interpreting Service* emblazoned across the front. He put it next to his plate and ordered a drink. An alcoholic drink. After looking at the menus and ordering our lunch, he pushed the legal-size portfolio stuffed with notes, receipts, and tax returns to my side of the table. "I feel your business has outgrown us," he said. "It would be prudent to hire another accounting firm, one closer to your headquarters."

He knew! He felt it! He somehow intuitively had knowledge of what I was about to say. He took the wind out of my sails, but also took the unpleasantness of me having to fire him away. I felt my shoulders lower and all the "girl guilt" slowly leave my body.

"Thank you," I whispered. "Thank you for taking that very young single mother all those years ago and convincing the owner of the business that you could teach her to do the job of a bookkeeper, and for literally pushing me into the position. I will never forget that, and it was a huge steppingstone in my professional life." I don't remember thanking him for the years he did the tax returns for my business, but I'm sure I did.

It was a big year. I had "fired" my bank and gone on to bigger and better. And now my CPA. Lessons that we need to constantly learn. Look at those outside advisors and remember who is paying for services, ask questions, and know when it's time to move on. I hope the takeaway on this is that, as women, we often don't want to offend anyone or not seem "nice," so we don't ask enough questions and don't move on when we should and end up leaving a lot of money on the table.

CHAPTER 40

What They Never Taught You in Business School

You don't have to be a business owner long to find out you will navigate situations no one ever prepared you for. As they say, you can't make this stuff up.

Our first office in downtown Syracuse was in a beautiful old Art Deco building that had fabulous marble floors and stunning architecture throughout. It had a parking garage attached for my staff and a restaurant on the first floor, both of which my employees appreciated. The problem with the building was that it was old and not being kept up very well, especially when it came to maintenance.

Often the elevators didn't work, or there was a leak somewhere, or the parking garage had concrete pieces that fell off the ceiling onto cars stored on the lower level. I negotiated and renegotiated my lease until I finally reached my limit the night I went to leave work and got stuck in the elevator. It was late at night, and all the staff had left. My husband was waiting for me to join him for dinner at a local restaurant. I grabbed all the books I was working on and headed for the fourth-floor elevator. I could hear the rain and thunder outside and pulled out my umbrella, to be ready for the rain.

As I entered the elevator and pushed the lobby button, there was a flash of light and then the doors closed as simultaneously the lights went out. None of the buttons in the elevator worked. Not the call button, not the emergency button. I was stuck in the dark with my hands full. It's funny how your mind works in those situations. I wasn't scared or panicked. I was pissed! I had put up with so much in this office space, from the water leaks that destroyed computers, to heat and air conditioning not working, and now to be stuck in this elevator alone late at night.

I grabbed my cell phone and called my CFO, as if complaining to her was going to solve anything. She called 911 for me and stayed on the phone, probably waiting for me to take hold of my predicament and freak out. While talking to her, I noticed a tiny sliver of light between the doors of the elevator and thought that if I could get something wedged in there, maybe I could open the door. I grabbed one of the binders I had and shoved the edge into the sliver of light. The doors moved just enough for me to get my fingers in the space and push the doors apart. I momentarily felt like a superhero! I grabbed all my belongings and rushed down the stairwell to my car. Once in my car, I realized that a lot could have gone wrong in the elevator and *why* did I think it was a good idea to put my hands in between doors that could have slammed shut at any moment? I texted my husband, who was still waiting at the restaurant, not knowing what had happened: *"Stuck in the elevator. Just got out. Order me a drink!"*

The next day, I called the landlord and told him I would only stay in the office suite if I was moved to a month-to-month agreement, and we voided our lease. He quickly agreed. However, I was soon to discover this was not the worst of my experiences in this space.

CHAPTER 41

Mice, Mice, and More Mice

About six months after the elevator experience, one of the buildings adjacent to our office was being demolished and readied for a new build. This property had sat vacant for decades and was in horrible condition. Everyone within sight of this building was happy to see it being torn down and excited for the new building to come.

Unfortunately, one of the side effects of this project was the disruption of thousands of mice who had moved in years ago and were now displaced. And in some sick twist of fate, they took shelter in our building. It started with stories from the first floor. An office worker finding a mouse scurrying around her desk one morning. A bank teller's story of how a mouse actually fell through the suspended ceiling on the first floor onto her counter one morning. And I can only imagine how many mice were now inhabiting the restaurant on that floor. However, I wasn't worried too much as we were safely on the fourth floor. Unless they came up the elevator, we were untouchable. Or so I thought.

A couple of months later, we were also inundated with mice. The landlord assured all of the tenants they were working on the problem and to their credit, every time we called, there were exterminators quickly in our suite. It became evident after a few weeks of this that they were only moving the mice from floor to floor, office space to office space, and that each "extermination" was quite temporary.

My office manager was on a mission. He went to the hardware store, bought peanut butter and several traps, and set the bait. Each night before he left, he set traps. And each morning, he arrived before the rest of the staff and emptied the traps. While we waited for the building management to solve the issue, we were trying our best to eradicate them from our suite, until they invaded our hallway during a contract negotiation.

A potential new customer was in the conference going over a contract with myself and my bookkeeper. We had joked about the mice and hoped they would stay behind the walls that day; we never saw one in daylight, only the evidence of them being there the next morning. However, they were about to make an entrance into the light of day.

As I sat at one end of our long conference table and my new customer at the other, my bookkeeper stood to gather some paperwork from her office. Upon her return, she stood in the doorway to the conference room and began a dialog with us inside. As she stood there, I noticed her eyes dart to the hallway. Sure enough, "they" were running up and down behind her as if in a foot race with invisible lines. My bookkeeper never blinked. We made eye contact and kept the conversation going. She coolly walked in the room and shut the door. I texted my office manager under the table with my cellphone on my lap—"MICE IN HALLWAY"—and that's all it took. He quickly rose, somehow made sure they were gone by the end of the negotiation, and by the time our new customers left the office, the "road was clear." The next week I signed a lease on a new build-out down the street and we were out of these offices within six months. No one prepares you for these things.

CHAPTER 42

The 4 Corners of Your Business

Earlier on, I mentioned the "four corners" of your business. Those integral people are your attorney, banker, insurance agent, and CPA. You will need all of these people in place at the onset of your business. It is crucial that each learns to understand your industry, or better yet, has experience working with a client within your industry. Be sure to interview at least three potential candidates in each "corner" before deciding on someone. Getting a referral from another business is fine, but remember that every business is different. Your particular personality is different, your learning curve will be different, and you will be schooled by each one along the way. The chemistry between you and the "expert" will be important. At the first gut feel that this might not be a fit for you, or if you see a red flag, move on!

1. Your CPA:
   - Have they worked with a business your size?
   - Are they approachable and will they answer your questions along the way?
   - Is an answer to a phone call, e-mail, or appointment billable? How much will it cost?
   - Ensure they are familiar with your particular accounting program.
   - How many times a year will they touch base with you?
     - Do not get caught up in a situation where your books are only looked at the end of the year and then you get blindsided with a huge tax liability on April 14.

o They should, at minimum, be preparing your taxes,
including your estimated payments, and touching base
with you twice a year.

My advice that they be approachable is so very important. Unless
you are a CPA yourself, you will have questions and, sometimes,
they will feel like ignorant questions that you're embarrassed to
ask, but you must ask them! You must be working with someone
who respects you and will answer your questions without being
judgmental or condescending. I've had that happen so many
times in the past from accountants—little jabs or comments that
left me feeling unwilling to ask questions in the future. They
need to stay in their lane while watching out for your business.

You have a right to ask questions and understand your
financials. You also have a right to be prepared for tax liability
and not have your feet kicked out from under you two weeks
before April 15, which happened to me one year. One April 2,
I received a call: "I hope you've squirreled away enough money
for this year. You owe $86,000, and don't forget on top of that
your first estimated for this year is also due on the April 15, so
that's another $28,000." When I finished picking myself up
off the floor, I stammered, "I don't have that kind of money
sitting in my checking account. What do I do?" To which
they replied, "*Well! You made enough money last year, what did
you do with it all?*" You don't need to be in that situation!

2. Your insurance agent:
   • You will need insurance, all kinds of insurance: workers'
   comp, general liability, professional liability, cyber security,
   and the list goes on. More than likely, you'll be using more
   than one insurance agent. I was lucky enough to find an
   agent who handled all of my insurance, except for the
   professional liability, and took the time to meet with me
   yearly to ensure my coverage was up to date and to explain
   each policy from cover to cover. He did not know my
   industry when we met; however, he took the time to get to
   know it so that I was never left exposed. A good agent will

find places you haven't thought of that need protection. Be sure to interview more than one agent and compare their suggestions so that you're not being "oversold" on coverage you do not need. And put it on your calendar to meet yearly to discuss your changing needs.

3. Your attorney:

- It is better to have someone in place who has familiarized themselves with you and your business than to have to search for a lawyer when something legal pops up. Find an attorney who is willing to meet with you and understand your industry. They will be able to proactively point out services you may need. My attorney for my business, James Baranello, has taken the time over the last 20 years to really understand my industry and has been there for me every step of the way. Specialists matter in the field of law, and he has referred me to them when needed: a trademark/copyright attorney, an Mergers & Acquisitions (M&A) attorney, and so on. Find someone that doesn't try to handle everything in house. Jim looks over all the BAAs (Business Associate Agreements), contracts for customers, and RFPs. He has drafted letters when needed to collect accounts receivable. Jim knows the industry and my business well enough to know what to look for and how to protect us. And he always responds within 24 hours. We got lucky.

4. Your financial person:

- As you've already read, it was Key Bank that literally rescued my business from a very bad position with a small credit union that was not built to do the type of commercial banking I needed. It may be fine to start with a small local credit union. Often, they are more open to doing business with a startup, but know when you've outgrown them. Find out about lines of credit and overdraft protection and understand *all* the fees. There will be things you never thought of when you opened your business, things you need to put in place quickly to run your business.
- For example, one day we found ourselves quickly needing to be able to handle overseas transactions, which Key Bank

handled without a hitch. Later, we wanted to do direct deposit for all our interpreters. Again, it was no problem. Ask about all these services beforehand and what the attached fees will be.

There is one "corner" that is also imperative for your financial peace: a financial advisor. If you are a sole proprietor, which most of us are, monies are very intertwined. You need someone to look at the health of your business *and* your personal finances. My financial advisor is OMC Financial. The owner, Cynthia Scott, has been instrumental in my financial success and the success of the business. She has helped me learn and navigate everything from investments to finding long-term care insurance. She has looked at the entire picture of my finances, taking into consideration how my business affects my income and vice versa. She's also been willing to be in contact with my CPA and insurance broker to help me navigate through some of the processes over the years. I highly recommend finding a financial advisor during your entrepreneurship journey.

Figure 42.1 Financial advisor, Cynthia Scott, and Theresa

Source: Photo credits to Sauro Photography

CHAPTER 43

Employee Issues

When I started my business, my first hire desperately needed employee benefits. I could not give them to her as a sole proprietor just starting out, so I turned to a staffing company for help. They offered to not only take care of payroll but to send potential employees my way. I was able to offer people benefit packages and have another entity take care of the bookkeeping. Having them take care of our payroll and staffing was wonderful, and still is to this day.

The really great thing about having a company such as the one I use, Staff Leasing, is the help they can offer when HR issues arise. Just like with the mice, there will be crazy situations you could never have imaged. One such was two former receptionists and their insane, insubordinate behavior. I'll call them Thelma and Louise. When my husband and I had purchased a commercial building to share, we also shared our bookkeeper and receptionists. When I moved to Syracuse and he took over the building himself, we split two receptionists. Thelma had been hired to work in Homer, where our commercial building stood. I still had an office there, so I was there, but seldom. On one of my visits, I mentioned the need of a receptionist for our expanding Syracuse office. Thelma excitedly told me about her friend, Louise, who needed a job and would love to work in Syracuse. And she offered to train her. Win–win, right? Wrong!

At that point in time, we were using IM (instant messenger) to communicate within our office space and between our offices in Homer and Syracuse. It was a quick and easy way to get information and messages back and forth. I would often IM the receptionist if I needed something done and my husband and I often communicated throughout the day with IM as well.

About the second month into hiring Louise for my Syracuse office, I started to have a bad gut feeling about her work ethic. And I will stop here to say, if there is any advice I can give to a business owner: *ALWAYS, ALWAYS, ALWAYS listen to that gut feeling!* I started to do a little digging after she left work and realized that not only was she not doing her job well, leaving many things unfinished each day, she was interestingly erasing all of her instant messages at the end of the day. I knew there was a setting for saving all the messages, so I went into the computer and changed that setting to "save." I also asked my husband to do the same with Thelma's IM on her computer in Homer.

That was on a Tuesday. That weekend, we looked at the messages on each computer. What we found was that both were not only constantly on IM with family, friends, and boyfriends, but with each other, and what they were saying about the staff and the businesses was the kicker. They were constantly gossiping about everything happening in both offices. The final straw was this line: *"Bob and Terre are so stupid; they have no idea that all we do is talk all day and don't even really have to work—hahahaha!"*

It was another "you can't make this up" moment as a business owner. Luckily, I had an HR backup in Staff Leasing and called them right away. Along with their legal advice on how to handle the firings, Bob and I had an idea of our own on how we wanted things to happen. We first let both Thelma and Louise know that we were having a meeting in the conference room of the Homer office that they needed to attend. We then printed out the multiple pages of IMs that had been going back and forth and highlighted the *"Bob and Terre are so stupid"* remark. We instructed our business manager to clean out their desks and put everything personal into boxes for them, so that we could hand them to each one on their way out the door.

The meeting was not pleasant. Louise burst into tears seeing the evidence of the IMs, while Thelma was enraged that we "invaded her privacy on HER computer" and insisted that we could not fire her. That was laughable. At that point, the representative from Staff Leasing took over the meeting and let both know that we certainly could fire them, that the computers did not belong to them, and that we had every right to look at the IM history. Ironically, years later, Bob and I ran into Thelma in the elevator at a hotel. She seemed almost excited to see us and chatted on about how she was doing and asked about employees at our businesses. I hope for the best for both young women, I really do. There was a reason we hired them, and it was painful to see the disrespect and lack of work ethic. However, we both recognized how young they were and hoped that they would take a sobering look at their actions in their future employment.

CHAPTER 44

Resources, Resources, Resources

Due to my delay in education, I jumped at any opportunity I could to become more educated about my industry and most of all running my company. One extremely helpful resource was Streetwise MBA, a program

Figure 44.1 Completion of the SBA's E200 class

run by the Small Business Association (SBA). They had a pilot program in Syracuse and were recruiting small business owners to partake.

There were more than a few women at the WPO who were interested. Unsure of the time it might take to get through the program, I cautiously attended the first session. I quickly learned that this program, Interise, was like a mini-MBA program. There were monthly meetings to attend, with an abundance of homework: dissecting your business model, setting goals, looking at your strengths and weaknesses, and being accountable to a small group you had been set up with to ensure success.

Each month they brought in experts: lawyers, CPAs, cyber security experts, and professors from Syracuse University who taught business administration and entrepreneurship. Although it was extremely time intensive, I began to have a new understanding of my business. I was looking at my financial statements differently. I was setting goals for my return on investment (ROI), dissecting each job and customer, and looking at my employees and their job descriptions closer.

The Interise program concluded with our instructor making personal visits to each of our offices. He did not sugarcoat his advice. I found I was doing a lot of things right by chance and not by design. However, there was a lot I needed to change and there were goals I needed to set. I will forever be grateful for the program and what I learned helped me become a stronger and more goal-oriented business owner. And the best part? It was, and still is, free. This program is still running, and you can find more information here: *https://interise.org/programs/*

There were many other resources that came across my desk over the years. The real trick is to sift through and see what is beneficial to running your business. There were some that were inspirational in nature, involving successful women who gave their success stories, and some that were only entertaining, a gathering of "Rah! Rah! I'm an entrepreneur, look at me run!" But those made me feel like I needed to be back at my desk working on my business, not sitting in a dining room somewhere patting myself on the back.

The idea is to be discerning and do some homework before you spend your time. If there was a program on how to read financial statements and have a better understanding of how the numbers impact your business,

I was signing up! If I found a presentation on HR and how to manage employees, I was also going. I learned what my weaknesses were and where to invest my time.

Don't waste your time learning what you know. Spend your time learning what your business needs you to know.

CHAPTER 45

Taking Calls in the Cooler at Wegmans

The one thing I didn't plan on when I started my business was that I would be on call 24/7, 365 days of the year. By the second year in, I had contracts that expected just that. So, I set up an emergency number, which was directed to my personal cell phone, changed my personal greeting to "You have reached the emergency number at Empire Interpreting Service," and carried it with me everywhere. Afraid to let it out of my sight and needing to live up to my obligations to provide interpreters whenever needed, round the clock, I had to be ready to answer my phone.

I brought it to the shower in the morning and more than once jumped out mid-shower to take a call and fill a request. It was with me at every meal, next to my knife and spoon, on silent but in my lap at church, at concerts, and at family holidays and events. And it was next to me on my nightstand every night. It was out of control and all consuming. And I realized this one day at Wegmans in the beer section.

Out grocery shopping on a Saturday afternoon, I received a text from my husband to pick up his favorite IPA. Standing at the cooler with my list in one hand and phone in the other, I was searching for his brand when my phone went off. I jumped back and knocked the phone out of my hand into the cooler. Terrified I'd miss a customer's call, I boldly walked through the swinging doors that read "EMPLOYEES ONLY" and fished through the back of the wire shelves and into cases of beer to retrieve my phone.

Collecting myself I said, "Empire Interpreting Service, how can I help you?" sending puffs of warm clouds into the cold refrigerated room. I grabbed a pen and started asking specifics, jotting them down on the backside of my grocery list: hospital name? Emergency Room (ER) or inpatient? Language needed? How soon? Call back number? When I finished, I saw people walking by peering in to see why this crazy lady was talking on her cell phone in the cooler.

I ditched my groceries, leaving a full cart in front of the beer section. I bolted to my car for privacy and filled the request, sending the correct language interpreter to the hospital, and confirming with the requestor. Walking back into the store, I realized just how out of hand this had gotten. The next Monday, I made a schedule within my small staff of alternating weeks that they would help me with the after-hour requests. As business owners, we are always on call 24/7 for *something*, and feel the need to be in control of everything. However, that day I learned just how out of control things had really become.

CHAPTER 46

"Oh My Dear, Where Are All Your Clothes?"

In 2007, my husband and I began building our forever home. It was a new building in downtown Syracuse in a quaint center of the city called Armory Square. The forever home would be a contemporary condo with all the amenities empty nesters would need while they each paid attention to their growing careers. The decision to downsize from our home 30 miles south was made in part because our boys were grown and had long since left home, and a lot of it was due to the growth of my business.

Our home sold much quicker than expected and we received an all-cash, no-contingency offer only if we moved in 30 days. That meant finding an apartment to live in while our condo was being built. Downsizing from our home into an apartment was one thing, but 12 months later, we were moving into a hotel room across the street from where our condo was being built as there were delays and postponements. The wait became excruciating.

Two years later, we were finally in our beautiful new contemporary condo. I couldn't be more in awe that we lived in this beautiful space with our balcony overlooking the square and a gorgeous fireplace, which I never wanted to turn off just because it looked so beautiful. I decided it was too good not to share and I held an open house; along with friends, I wanted to share my good fortune with the women of the WPO. I had built strong business and personal ties with them and still looked forward to our monthly meetings at which I learned so much about being a female entrepreneur.

One of the things I was most proud of was my walk-in closet. I had never had a walk-in closet before and although it was smallish and narrow, it was most definitely a walk-in. During the touring of my condo, I took each woman to the closet as I knew women especially would appreciate my excitement.

One of the women in the WPO, who I highly admired, was a woman with a very successful financial business. She was always dressed impeccably, with every hair in place, and seemed to have the air of Princess Grace. She had also started her business alone as a single mom, and I was always so impressed by her perseverance and resilience. When she walked into a room, her entire demeanor exuded professionalism and success.

As I proudly took her to the door of my walk-in, she looked around and smiled. "This is beautiful, my dear, but where *are* all your clothes?" I lied and said some things were still in storage and quickly closed the closet door. The next morning, I revisited my closet and took stock of what she meant. There was a shoe rack big enough to carry 50 pairs of shoes, but there were five pair on the rack, which included a pair of sneakers and a pair of boots. My suits looked like rejects of Hilary Clinton's pantsuits, all dark blue and black, with only white shirts to accompany them. It did not look like a successful businesswoman's closet.

What it did look like was my past. As a sign language interpreter, we wear solid dark colors so that our hands can be easily seen against a dark background. Interpreters of color should wear solid white or light colors. What I had assembled was a closet that looked like I was going to nothing but funerals. All black. All white blouses. Two pairs of shoes. Flats. Not good. I wasn't sure where to turn, but I didn't have to look far.

CHAPTER 47

Introductions to Mr. Weitzman and Ms. Carlisle

After my closet "incident," I decided to call on Ms. Fashion Plate from the WPO and boldly ask for fashion recommendations for things that would say, "I'm a successful business owner" and not "I'm on my way to a funeral."

Cynthia was more than excited to help! We made plans to go shopping at her favorite places in and around Syracuse and soon after made plans for trips to NYC! She was to be my "image consultant."

Cynthia was extremely kind while also being brutally honest, pointing out to me that I was always a representation of my business, whether going to meet a client or grocery shopping at Wegmans. She also pointed out to me that one of my business suits, which all looked alike, was the one in a photo of myself on the shelf of my office, taken 10 years prior. Ouch! What she didn't know was that I had worn that suit for many years before the photo had even been taken.

Living paycheck to paycheck most of my adult life, it never occurred to me that you replaced clothes before they fell apart or if they became too big or small. It also never occurred to me that now my perspective on clothes needed to change. My appearance, or more precisely the money I put into my appearance, was no different than the money I put into making sure I had an office or a website that looked professional and successful. I was not reflecting success back to the world via my wardrobe. So, onto the introductions!

Cynthia introduced me to clothing lines like Carlisle, Perse, and Lafayette 148 that she purchased directly from a consultant who helped you put clothes and accessories together that best reflected the image you wanted to portray. I learned about tailoring: everything must be tailored to fit?! What did I know? I thought off the rack anywhere other than Target was high end!

She introduced me to the owners of a shoe store outside the city, Paul Karaz Shoes, which is where I still order all my shoes, and I was introduced to the likes of Stuart Weitzman, Anyi Lu, and Brenda Zaro. And there I learned that your shoes could look beautiful and be functional, tailored to your feet, stretched, and altered to your specifications.

I started to feel successful in these new clothes. I paid attention to things like manicures, pedicures, and my hair. I realized that looking like I put zero thought into how I looked was not good for business. I got over the fact that any money spent on nice clothing was "selfish." It was business. The first impression people get of your business is many times the impression of you.

The way you look is an investment in you. It is a business expense, although not tax deductible. It is an expense you should plan for. Clothes have the power of making you feel bad about yourself or empowered to walk into a board room and negotiate. Make the investment. It will help you grow your business and your self-esteem.

CHAPTER 48

When Real Life Intrudes

As I mentioned earlier, I lost my dad right before I decided to start my business. During his illness, he mentioned to my siblings and myself that our mom was forgetting things and to keep an eye on her. I brought it up to her doctor, who quickly dismissed it as the stress of knowing she was losing her husband of 50 years. It was a relief to all of us, as we had our hearts overwhelmed with losing our dad. Unfortunately, the doctor was wrong. And as what often happens with women, a serious illness was dismissed as my mother being overly wrought and emotional.

On the heels of going through 18 months of torture slowing losing our dad, we were now facing the loss of our mother, painfully and incrementally, to a very cruel form of dementia, Lewy Body Disease. I luckily lived very close in the beginning of my mother's illness. I thought I could handle whatever my mom's needs were and I was determined to keep her in her house for as long as possible. I was so wrong on both fronts. The next few years were grueling, heart-wrenching years for the entire family.

I was made responsible for the financial decisions, which was a blessing and a curse. I made good and bad mistakes. I was given mostly bad advice from outsiders which, coupled with my determination to keep her in her home, only postponed the inevitable. Both my sister and I tried to arrange to have her come live with us and care for her. Both of us realized within hours it was not a workable solution. She needed 24/7 care for her to stay safe. Eventually, she was placed in a senior center with a dementia unit.

During the time we were grappling with mom's illness, I moved my headquarters 45 minutes away. This was during the years my business was growing the fastest, while simultaneously my mom's illness progressing the quickest. I was working until 6 p.m. or 7 p.m. and then jumping in my car and driving 45 minutes to the senior center, which was near her home and her friends, other children, and grandchildren. And then 45 minutes back, late into the evening hours.

To say this didn't affect the way I ran my business would be a lie. I remember going into staff meetings and thinking, "We must make X amount of dollars, bottom line, in order to take care of Mom," and I was pushing harder and harder to gain new customers all the while refusing to give up control on responsibilities I really needed to push aside for a season. I was so driven that I literally set up a quasi-office at the foot of her death bed in the end and kept up my frantic pace there for the few weeks while she lay unconscious, dying. I honestly could not stop this absurd behavior, spurred on by all the responsibilities and the overlapping grieving of losing my parents.

Family tragedies and crises will come while you are building your business. They will interject in a way you cannot imagine. Not being prepared not only will be devastating for you personally but can also be dangerous for your business. I was lucky. My business kept flourishing. I had the money I needed to do my best to take care of my mom's expenses, but I was giving up precious moments with her I can never get back.

For the sake of yourself and your business, be prepared ahead of time. Have a contingency plan. Have a trusted employee as backup for everything that is critical to the business, so they can take care of things if you are unavailable. Make sure someone else can approve payroll, sign checks, sign contracts, and make executive decisions in your absence. Everything from passwords to programs and the combination to the office safe need to be put somewhere accessible to that one person. Make sure your attorney and liaison at your bank have the information in writing of who that person is.

Most importantly, take time off when family crises come. I am embarrassed to say the day my father died, I still tried to go to work. That was during my freelancing days. It was ridiculous. I was in no shape to drive; much less be out interpreting. And, on Christmas Eve in 2009, when I walked out of my mother's room with a box of her belongings and headed to the hospital garage in the dark early hours of the cold winter morning, there was no one there with me. My heart was full of self-loathing for bad decisions and regret. I had closed myself off in my thinking I could "do it all," take care of my mother, and keep running my business. We are not machines. We are replaceable at our office if we have carefully planned for our absence. We are not replaceable to our loved ones.

CHAPTER 49

Superglued Dentures

One thing I can relate to is the inability to access health care or basic goods and services that you need. Bottom line, I can relate to being poor. One of the nice things about having money is being able to do things for people that can really change their quality of life. I believe that as women, we want to be caretakers and fix things for people. I know I tend to try to jump in and fix things with money and often make things worse for others or for myself. And when this happens in the workplace, it can mean you are overstepping in the face of trying to do something nice. An example is superglued dentures.

For many years, I had a male receptionist. He wasn't my first choice, but my protocol with new hires in the office was to pick my top three people and then let my staff meet them in an informal group interview that I did not attend. When I needed a new receptionist, I had whittled it down to two young women and a middle-aged man I'll call David. My staff loved David. I must admit, although he wasn't the most qualified, I had been drawn to his easy laugh and laid-back personality. So it was to be. David was hired.

A few months after David was hired, I surprised him in the break room. I quickly came around the corner and he was in front of a small mirror that was hung behind the door. David was holding his dentures in one hand and a bottle of Super Glue in the other. I tried not to react. I had never noticed he wore dentures, but ended up blurting out, "What in the world are you doing?"

"My dentures broke again. I'll have them fixed in a minute and get back to work." I stopped and slowly said, "*You're supergluing your dentures?* Do you need to go to the dentist? You can go. It's okay." I secretly wanted him to get this taken care of but in the privacy of a dental office and not our break room.

David's normally happy face dropped, and I knew the look only too well. I'd had it on my face many times in my life. It is embarrassing to not be able to afford something other people could never imagine, like not having enough money for food, or rent, or health care—or new dentures.

I quickly went to the phone and called one of the members of the WPO who happened to be a dentist and she immediately agreed to fit David into her schedule that day. I'm not sure if I handled it well. I'm sure David was somewhat embarrassed, but I sent him out the door to her office—dentures and Super Glue in hand. And when he was told he would need a full set of new dentures, I assured him I would take care of it. Years later, David suddenly left the company. However, I will never regret buying him a new pair of dentures that didn't hurt his mouth. That he didn't have to superglue together, and I chalked that up to one of the spiffs of being a successful businesswoman.

CHAPTER 50

Keeping Sight of Why We Do What We Do

Sitting in your office every day, navigating the responsibilities of running a business, you can lose sight of the end result. Talking to customers, meetings with accountants, lawyers, bankers, and staff. You are often removed from that product or service being provided right outside your company doors.

As a language service provider, we understand our job is to facilitate communication. We comprehend that bridge from source to target language, and we've felt and seen that moment when two parties can fluently communicate. We have that rare opportunity to see how effective interpretation affects people's lives.

However, it often gets forgotten in those long hours of managing the day-to-day. On one of my busiest days ever, I was interrupted and jerked into the reality of what we do by a phone call. It went something like this:

Intercom: "Terre, you have a phone call ... can you take it?"
Me: "I'm s-o-o-o busy ... is it important?"
Intercom: "I think so ... it's somebody's mother"

Okay, that stopped me. In my madness of the 12-hour day and the piles of responsibilities, papers, e-mails, and financial statements I was poring through, I started to laugh. "Somebody's mother? That's like half the world, right? No name, just 'somebody's mother.'" My curiosity got the best of me; if this was a new way to get sales calls through to me, it was genius.

It so happens it was the mother of one of the students we provide interpreting services to in a small rural high school. The mother was choking back tears as she told me the story of her child's struggle through the educational process that was taught in a language different from their own. She told me of the difference our interpreter had made: how this student was for the first time on the honor roll and playing sports, making friends, and excelling in school. She had called to thank me for the service we provided and for "starting the company in the first place." That was a stunner. No one had ever said those words to me before. "Thank you for starting the company *in the first place.*"

Now, I'm aware that this child's success had as much to do with a loving, supportive family and a school system that valued effective communication for their students as it had to do with myself and my interpreters, but it made me put my pen down, push my keyboard away, and contemplate the end result of what we did, the "small changes" that we made outside our office doors.

And knowing that some kid out there was having a happier experience in school, well, that's pretty great.

CHAPTER 51

Incompatible With Your Customer

There are going to be those times when you actually dread seeing a customer's number pop up on your phone. When you should be happy to see calls coming in and orders being placed. However, that phone number pops up and you cringe. Is it time to part ways even though they make your cash register ring?

It may be. There are many times you need to re-evaluate your customers especially if you find that you don't want to talk to them. Customers that are cringe-worthy are worth taking a hard cold look at.

First, what are some of the mistakes we may be making as a vendor of services for that customer that would make you recoil from contact with them?

1. **You are providing a service or product outside of your expertise.** This often happens when a business is young. You want so much to produce revenue and increase sales that you go outside of your area of expertise and try to make something work. You will end up frustrating your customer and expending too much time and energy on this product or service that you never intended to provide in the first place. BE HONEST. Let your customers know you do not provide the service or product and move on. Trying to provide something you know little about or have few resources for can ruin your reputation.

2. **The customer is extremely high maintenance.** This is when you need to know your numbers. Are you netting $50 on a project that took you 6 phone calls and 18 e-mails to provide? Every business owner should know what each hour of their time costs. Monetize

your time, and then decide if this customer is really a good fit for you.

3. **When they don't pay, or they pay extremely slowly.** Again, monetize the time of your staff. Is your bookkeeper spending one to two hours each month trying to collect from a customer? Are you going into your line of credit to pay for supplies or employees while you repeatedly wait for this customer to pay you? Time to rethink the customer or have them pay upfront.

4. **The customer makes phishing calls.** This means that every call is a series of calls to you and your competitors to see who will come in with the lowest price. These take time and money. If you are constantly being asked for quotes and cost reductions, you may want to rethink this customer. While this may be very worthwhile with a large contract, it may be a complete financial black hole for a one-hit wonder. The truth may be that you are just not a good fit.

Incompatibility can reduce your profits, make your employees miserable, and suck your time. Know who you want to do business with, who you can create a good partnership with, and who you can provide an excellent service or product to.

CHAPTER 52

Trying to Be Everything for Everyone

One of the biggest mistakes I've made was trying to fulfill every customer's need or request. Some of the costly mistakes I made were offering language classes, having a mini bookstore with texts on language and interpreting, and providing voiceovers for Public Service Announcements (PSAs).

We delivered on all of those items, but at a large financial cost. I learned in my third year of business that I needed to stay in my lane and find my "sweet spot" of what we did really well and what things we were actually making money on.

This is not to say that we haven't expanded the services we offer. We started providing American Sign Language (ASL) interpreters on site. About three years in, we were getting calls for spoken languages. I was intrigued and wanted to expand another dimension to the business. Eventually we did, and today we offer on-site spoken and sign language interpreters. We provide interpreters on demand over the phone and virtually. We also have a department that takes care of written translations of anything from legal documents to entire websites.

I believe we are now in our "sweet spot" as a language service provider. We communicate for our customers in several modalities. We decline requests for services we don't currently provide, and we make sure to "stay in our lane."

CHAPTER 53

Multiple Locations

When I first started the business, it was in my home office. Six months later, I moved into a very small office on the second floor of a multi-purpose building on Main Street in Cortland. On the main floor was a coffee shop, the Blue Frog. It was a "crunchy granola" coffee shop with organic coffee and guitar players on the weekends. Tapestries hung from the corners, and it looked like it had been awkwardly transplanted into this old building that had in the 1950s served as the home to a very large hardware store.

Across from the Blue Frog was a Subway restaurant. The smell from the Subway permeated the building every morning. By noon, it was mixed with the smell of hair perms from Connie's, the hair salon perched kitty-corner from my office on the second floor. There were two or three other small offices that were rented out by individual therapists or advisors of some sort.

This office had three rooms. In one was my desk; it was across from a small waiting area; and then there was a small conference room and a tiny office behind mine. This is where I would remain for the next year. Here, Stacey, my first hire who is now my CFO, would work with me to build the business.

Simultaneously as I was starting my business, my husband was looking for a larger place to move his psychotherapy office. The idea came to us to possibly buy a commercial building and share the space. We purchased a beautiful old Victorian building in the village of Homer, which sits shoulder-to-shoulder with Cortland. We restored and recreated a neglected but charming building over the next year. I loved working in that building. The train ran by throughout the day as the tracks were very close to the edge of the property, and at times it drowned out phone conversations with customers. But it had a beautiful charm with large lawns and flowers edging the perimeter. It was wonderful.

Figure 53.1 Building in Homer, NY, purchased to house my business

As the business grew, it became evident that most of our customers were now coming from the Syracuse area. I really felt it was important to have a Syracuse address and the decision was made to move my son Jay, who was now working for me, to a small office in downtown Syracuse to have a presence there. It was small, but nicely laid out with a reception area, a break room, one large office, and a conference room. Jay got to work making contacts with interpreters and customers, and we were now a multilocation company.

We grew some more. Corissa came on board right out of college and was eager to help expand the company. She created a spoken language department; up to this point, we were only offering sign language services. She moved into the reception area of Jay's office and had to literally squeeze between a wall and the side of the desk to get in and out of this tiny space. We used to joke that it was a good thing she was petite, or she wouldn't be able to work there. Corissa worked her magic, and we were gaining customers.

It was obvious we would need more staff for EIS, and the Syracuse office was maxed out. I was still working in Homer with Stacey. As my business was growing, so was my husband's practice. He was hiring social workers to see clients as his waiting list was long and he saw an opportunity to expand and move to a business model where he oversaw other therapists. They also needed room to serve clients.

Around this time, my oldest son, Trevor, was looking for work in Charlotte, NC Sensing his frustration and sensing an opportunity, I thought, "Why do I have this business where I'm hiring strangers, when I could offer my son who is struggling to find a job?" I also had a bit of "multilocation fever" and thought this could be another way to grow the company. Trevor found an office in the SouthPark area of Charlotte in a beautiful, shared office co-op and went to work.

This was all way before virtual work was popular and VoIP phones were also not offered yet, so we had multiple phone numbers and were using iChat through our Mac computers to communicate what we had no way to intercom each other.

Then we received our first job in New York City. This was the big time. If you can make it here, you can make it anywhere, right? So, I was off and setting up another office. It was a tiny office where you could barely squeeze behind the desk and the wall, in a high rise across from Penn Station. We had a shared secretary and a conference room where you could schedule usage. We now had a Manhattan phone number and a secretary to take our calls and messages. We rarely went there. It basically sat unused. I did travel to NYC a few times, but rarely used the office when I was there. I discovered that in the city most business transactions were happening in restaurants, at lunch tables, or over a drink after hours, not in an office or conference room. This office was a huge, unnecessary, money suck.

But, I now had four addresses and four different phone numbers at the end of my name on my e-mail and on my letterhead. I had let myself become so misguided by the thought that I needed to have all this brick and mortar to grow my business and at a huge cost to the business. A mortgage on the place in Homer and rents on three other locations. It was a sign of the times, the early 2000s. Businesses grew by adding addresses. It was a deep trap that I fell into.

One by one those offices were closed, and by 2016 we were completely virtual. One office space alone was costing me $125K per year in rent, utilities, parking, supplies, and a full-time receptionist. Don't let old school thinking and your ego get in the way of sound business practices. An expense of $125,000 was a lot of ego I could do without.

CHAPTER 54

The Longer You Work in Someone Else's Shadow, the Longer Before You Can Cast Your Own

Both of my sons work in my business. Both had a very different pathway to working with me. Neither ever set out to be part of the business; life just happened, and here we were. There are many, many challenges to working with family and having family work for you. There are many, many wonderful things about working together, but just as many land-mines to avoid. Hopefully, my experiences will help you think about or rethink hiring family.

My youngest son, Justin (or Jay, which is what he's gone by since college), went to Messiah College in Pennsylvania with plans to go on to graduate school afterwards. The summer after graduation, he and some buddies drove to West Virginia to celebrate a professional milestone of their residential director. While on the trip, he suffered serious injuries in an accident that meant months of treatments and surgeries.

Jay moved back home and started receiving treatments. Physically and emotionally beaten down and without the support system of his close friends from college that had been his family for four years, he was in limbo and unable to plan for graduate school.

Once his injuries were addressed and, physically, he was healed, I asked him if he'd like to make some money working for me a few hours a week on a marketing idea I had. He reluctantly agreed. I think he did it more to help me out than anything. I was happy to see him out of the house and around people again, and the marketing strategy was working. Jay was in the office more and more, and with the success of his visits and the positive feedback I was getting from customers, I decided to offer him a permanent, full-time position. To my surprise, he accepted. That was in 2004 and he is now about to enter his 20th year with EIS.

The marketing idea I had was to put together packets for medical facilities to target the emergency rooms of every hospital within driving distance and let them know of our services. His instructions were to put on a suit, walk into the ER, and hand the person at the desk our packet, listing all of the languages we provided with a laminated card that had double-sided tape on the back so they could easily post and reference it, and to only say, "I've been asked to leave this with you," and nothing more. We acquired several new customers that year due to Jay's persistence and the many miles he put on his old Jeep Wrangler.

Watching Jay grow into his role at Empire has been intriguing. It does not escape me that he has put his dreams aside to make mine come to fruition. He has had starts and stops with the company but has stayed with us and been a huge part of its success. He came up with the idea of developing our own proprietary software system that allowed us to schedule interpreters and track jobs in a way that no one else was doing, in a way that is now industry standard. He has a knack for looking hard at numbers and thus looking out for the company when sometimes I let my emotions get in the way. He is well liked by other staff and has the respect of our customers. I truly hope that someday soon Jay will be able to pursue his dreams with the same drive that he has helped me pursue mine.

My other son, Trevor, has lived in North Carolina since he left home. He met his now wife there and they decided to make Charlotte their home to be near her family. In 2006, Trevor and I were having a conversation about his recent job hunt. He had been working for a company that had recently closed and was having a difficult time finding something else. He was becoming exhausted and frustrated with his search. After one such conversation, I hung up the phone and contemplated how I could help. I'm definitely a "fixer" and wanted to give him some pearls of advice, but I knew the job market and understood what he was facing. And then it dawned on me. *Why was I working so hard to build this business and what was it all for? For my family! Duh!* I quickly put a plan together to expand into the Charlotte area and offered Trevor a job as a director of sales for the North Carolina region.

The office in Charlotte opened and then closed within two years as we all moved to virtual work. Trevor's role changed a couple of times over the years as the business grew. He is now our director of social media, along with coordinating all our emergency services for customers needing 24/7 responses. Much like his brother, his life goal was not to be working for his mom. However, he is extremely loyal to the business and loves working with our interpreters. His vision for how the website and our social media could impact the business has moved our business forward in multiple ways. We now receive 95 percent of all new requests directly through our website that Trevor maintains.

There are wonderful things about having both your sons work with you. The best part is that I talk to them daily, sometimes several times a day. Not many mothers have that luxury of touching base with their kids daily once they're grown and out on their own. I know more about them, their spouses, and their children as I am privy to that constant contact. It's pretty wonderful.

Now the negatives. Because we all work for the same company and the company is small, having family time on holidays and family vacations is almost impossible. Remember, even though hundreds of interpreters work for us, there is only a staff of five in the office running the day-to-day operations. Taking all three of us out is impossible. Consequently, we try to stagger our vacations. When we do all get together or celebrate holidays together, one or more of us is usually still working in the background.

There was a time when I was being highly pressured to sell the business by a potential buyer who had contacted me out of the blue. My business was not for sale; however, this company was making a very attractive offer. I talked to the boys about it and the response was, "it would just be great for you to just be 'Mom' and not be our boss." It was a little heartbreaking to hear that. They were right. Even when we were not working, we talked about work. Even when we were celebrating birthdays or holidays, work was looming in the background. It pushed me to seriously consider the offer. I eventually decided not to sell, but it hit home that they were both ready to cast their own shadow.

CHAPTER 55

A Space Pioneer

In 2018, I was interviewed for a podcast via Encore Interview by Forbes Books. During the podcast, the interviewer called me a "space pioneer." It was in relation to my choice to get rid of the offices, which I did, one by one over the years, and take my company virtual long before working virtually was even a thought.

It all started when Corissa, my Director of Spoken Languages, entered my office choking back tears. She was recently engaged and was going to move to Virginia soon. She was giving her notice, but clearly did not want to leave the company. I asked her to let me think about how she might still be able to be connected to Empire Interpreting Service. As she left my office, I looked at my desk and my phone. We had recently switched to "Voice over the Internet" phones (VoIP) and my mind started turning. I did not want to lose this employee, for so many reasons.

At that moment, it occurred to me that Corissa could take her phone with her, plug it into a home office in Virginia, and continue working for us. I immediately second-guessed myself, thinking that this was a crazy idea. I called the VoIP company and asked if she could still intercom with us? "Yes!" Would it work with her home Internet, was it safe? "Yes!" Would it cost me more? Is there anything I'm not thinking of that would make this an untenable idea? "No!"

Not yet convinced that this was a good idea, I asked other business owners for their feedback. There was honestly a lot of negative feedback. "How will you know if she's actually working?" "How will you keep company information safe?" "How would you get your computer back if she leaves the company?" All of their questions and responses were pretty negative.

Did I want to let her go? Part of my heart was being pulled. I had worked with her from when she started as a wide-eyed and enthusiastic college grad to her role now as a department director, responsible for creating and growing a department, managing dozens of interpreters, writing RFPs. She was respected and loved by all of us. I wanted her to stay more than I would worry about any of the naysayers. It was 2012. No one was doing this. Yet. But we were about to.

When I told my story to the interviewer at Forbes, he said, "Wow! You were truly a space pioneer." Long before virtual work became a thing, we were leading the way. Eventually all my staff moved to working at home. As each office closed, it saved the company hundreds of thousands of dollars in overhead. And when COVID hit eight years later, we already knew how to work virtually. We didn't have the overhead of many of our competitors, there was no learning curve, and I truly believed this saved us.

CHAPTER 56

Navigating Running Your Business From a Home Office

During the summer, I worked from our vacation home on Cazenovia Lake. The rest of the year, I worked from our condo in downtown Syracuse, in a beautiful new build that we downsized to after our kids left home. It was a small but workable condo for the two of us, but there was no designated office space. I turned a corner next to the dining room table into another makeshift office. It was dark. I felt as if I never had a moment away from the business as it was glaring at me from my living space. I was missing my staff terribly. I hated working from home. I missed the camaraderie I felt the last 15 years having my staff around me. The casual conversation and the brainstorming. The next year dragged on for me.

It was about this time of feeling lost while trying to get my bearings professionally and personally that sent me to a therapist. I was trying to juggle my growing business with taking care of my mom when she was so ill, and I had employee issues that I needed help navigating. Having a therapist to talk to can often help you discover why you react to personnel issues and talk through your fear of failure, expanding, and how to navigate being a business owner. I highly recommend you have one in your back pocket.

In my session with her, while discussing my feelings of isolation, she stopped me and said, "Where's your heart? Where are you truly happy?" I blurted out, "When I'm with my kids."

An "Aha" moment ... I decided to sell everything in New York in order to purchase properties close to my kids. I purchased a small townhome in North Carolina and a condo in Philadelphia, with the idea to split my time and be close to both of my sons as much as possible.

I furnished both with a separate office. Not in the corner in the dark. Not crammed into a tiny office that is super uncomfortable and unworkable. A separate office with a desk, file cabinets, shelving. Windows to look out of and a door that you close at the end of your workday. I truly feel like I "got it right."

I also keep the same 8 a.m. to 5 p.m. schedule. I dress for work as if I was going to my old office on the top floor of that beautiful building. I have shoes on. Yes, that makes a difference! For me, I cannot negotiate contracts, deal with employee issues, and interview interpreters in a pair of jeans. What I wear determines how I feel about myself. How I respect myself and my business. Not to say there aren't people out there that can run their billion-dollar businesses in jeans and a t-shirt. Obviously, there are, but know yourself and how you can still feel like a business owner while working from home.

Make your office space beautiful and workable. Even if others can't see it, it reflects you and your business. You need to be comfortable and have everything around you that you need. I hired California Closets to help me utilize the space in my Philadelphia condo. It's beautiful and functional and I face windows on two sides that give me a view of the streets below. I don't feel isolated here as I'm in the middle of a busy and energetic city.

Get outside help to assist with making your office all it can be, such as an interior designer or a specialist in offices like I had with California Closets. I've also used the designers at Ethan Allen when purchasing furniture from them. It's a free service and they'll come to your home and map out what will work for you. Have an office you want to walk into each morning and one that energizes you throughout your day. And ultimately, it's good for business.

CHAPTER 57

Memberships and Boards

There will be professional memberships that you can and should be a part of as a business owner. As a freelance interpreter, I was always a member of the RID (Registry of Interpreters for the Deaf), the NAD (National Association of the Deaf), and NAJIT (National Association of Judicial Interpreters and Translators). Once I started the business, I still belonged, but now on an organizational membership level. Professional memberships had a very different meaning when I was a freelance interpreter. They offered professional development, sanctioned my CEUs, and offered conferences and networking in a field where we often work in isolation.

At an organizational membership level, they offer information on trends in our industry and networking on a different level, often with other language service providers. They also provide an opportunity to present yourself on topics and share your experiences and expertise as a business owner. I believe in keeping my certifications current and staying a member as a show of support and respect to my interpreters and to the communities that we serve.

As I grew my business, I quickly realized the importance of networking and promoting my company. The first time I was invited to be part of a different organization, a private club, was when a member of the WPO extended an offer to join a local Syracuse social club, the Century Club. It was formed in 1866 initially as an association for literary and recreational purposes. It is now a place for social and business gatherings and is filled with local businesspeople, doctors, lawyers, and socialites. I had been to various events at the Century Club for fundraisers and business luncheons, always invited as a guest.

I was in awe that anyone would consider inviting me to such a place. There was a sponsor, the person who initially invited me to join, and then paperwork about me and my business. Next came a kind of "meet and greet" with some board members, some members at large, and my sponsor. We had drinks in a beautiful historic room with a large fireplace on one side and a piano on the other. I felt unworthy and out of place, but I knew this would be an important opportunity for my business. I was voted in and began my time at the Century Club.

I loved the offerings of special events and ability to host business events at the club. I often stopped by for breakfast on the way to my office, just to take in the beauty of the venue and soak in the fact that I was part of such a place in this historic building. I wondered if my dad would be proud. Or would he think it a bit haughty? I must admit, I loved that the staff knew me by name, the bartender kept my favorite Italian wine stocked for my visits, and the chef would create "to go" dinners for me to pick up when my husband and I were working until midnight. It was truly lovely to be a member and it reinforced to me that all my hard work had paid off in a way that made me feel accepted.

The return on investment (ROI) of club membership dues and fees was probably not as healthy as the ROI I felt just being a member. Does ego play a part in being a business owner? Absolutely!

The next group I was invited to be a member of was a board for a community organization that served the members of the community by offering social events and educational events. It seemed another prestigious group and I was waiting to be vetted by the members. I mentioned this to my financial advisor, proud that another esteemed group was about to "deem me worthy." Her reply stopped me in my tracks. "Do you know how much they expect you to commit to yearly in order to keep your seat?"

This was not something I had even considered. Along with monthly meetings and expected time on different committees, there was a $25,000 per year gifting expectation that went along with your board seat. I got knocked down several pegs. I evaluated the cost to my time and where I would like to put $25K in giving. I graciously declined the invitation, gave them a one-time donation, and moved on.

And so it went over the past 20 years. Picking and choosing what memberships you should have, boards you should serve on, and there are many, is a learned exercise. Choose the ones that you believe in, that have meaning to you personally, or the communities you serve. Choose the ones that will benefit your business, not just your ego. Good networking, educational opportunities, or just ways to give back to your community.

For me, that has been the Union League in Philadelphia, where I now live. The realtor who sold me my condo, Kristin Daley, another entrepreneur, and very successful businesswoman, mentioned the Union League to me. She was a member and thought it would be a great way for me to make connections in a city where I was a stranger to everyone. There was a process, a long process, as this is a very prestigious and historic club, ranked the Number 1 City Club in America. The Union League was founded in 1862 as a patriotic society to support the Union and the policies of President Abraham Lincoln. The Union League of Philadelphia laid the philosophical foundation for other Union Leagues across a nation torn by civil war. The League has hosted U.S. presidents, heads of state, industrialists, entertainers, and dignitaries from around the globe and has proudly supported the American military in each conflict since the Civil War. The Union League continues to be driven by its founding motto, *Amor Patriae Ducit*, or "Love of Country Leads."

I was fascinated by this club and attended several times as a guest before applying for membership. The philosophies of this club were something I held dear. The opportunities for fellowship with other Philadelphians along with learning from prominent business leaders were something I wanted and needed. Unfortunately, my application was stalled during COVID. However, as of this writing, I have been a member for three years and see the ROI on this investment in many ways. I belong to the Business Leadership Forum, the Entrepreneur Roundtable, and the Broad Street Bulls investment group.

Being a member of this club has helped me grow as a person and as an entrepreneur and allowed me to be in audience to some of the most successful businesspeople and community leaders in the country. I finally got it right. And you will, too. Do your research. Don't let your ego get in the way or be flattered by invitations to boards that will deplete your time and wallet. **Go where you can give back and get back as a business leader.**

CHAPTER 58

The Names Behind the Paychecks

My weeks are filled with multiple conversations with interpreters and staff. Normally, the dialog of business involves interpreting assignments or catch-up meetings with staff. However, one week seemed unusually melancholy. Conversations were taking on new meaning. There was a smattering of good news, but I had heard a lot of bad as well during my nonstop Monday through Friday.

When I entered my office late on that Friday, I saw my bookkeeper had left me a tall stack of checks to sign. Exhausted from the week and wanting to get this last task done before mail pick up, I plopped myself in my chair and rolled it up to my desk. As I thumbed through the list of interpreter checks to go out, I couldn't help but be transported back to those conversations that had affected my end-of-week mood. The good and bad news. The discussions with those who worked with me.

What usually was just a long list of names became another list, a list of real-life events. As I signed each check, I was reminded of those earlier conversations.

- The interpreter whose mother had just passed away. Her amazing grace in such a moment, her thankfulness for those who supported her, and her concern for her work commitments.
- The interpreter who had overwhelming family problems. His voice reflected a heart being ripped from his chest. I'm not even sure how all the conversations began, but they ended in my heart being broken for him. Yet, his concern was that he remained focused on his jobs at hand.

- The staff who received digital images of his unborn daughter, with all the joy and anticipation that goes hand-in-hand. Reveling in the love for something not yet seen or touched.
- A translator who received a dire prognosis telling me he needed to take time off. He emotionally fell like a precariously built deck of cards, toppling one by one into a pool of desperation.
- An interpreter who discovered that for days she'd been walking on a broken ankle. Amazed at her tolerance for pain, her words hit me. "I can work. It's not a problem, I can work!"

A long list of names, many I could not pronounce, some I could not remember to put a face to, but all deeper than the list of reductions in our bank account. They emptied and filled my heart with their stories, their spirit, their despair, and their delight. And as I signed the last check and pushed back in my chair, their names remained in my head and in my soul.

My lesson: never forget that while I am responsible for every paycheck, behind those numbers is larger responsibility. To always be mindful that there is a human being in each name. Someone loved by others. Someone loving others. Someone going through something while still working. For me. *That* should be etched in *my* mind and heart. Every single day.

CHAPTER 59

Clichés Have Meaning

I've been accused of being a workaholic, a compulsive entrepreneur, even a Scrooge, a money counter. Someone more interested in poring over financial statements than joining the "real world." There is a lot of truth to that statement. I've been poor. Dirt poor. Food stamp poor. And like anyone who shares my experiences, I worry that someday my livelihood will mysteriously disappear.

Success has no bearing on those fears. I need to know I have financial security. I won't apologize for that. I remember days when there was no money for food, for a home. For warmth. I won't ever go back there. And neither will my staff and interpreters as long as I have breath in my body. However, there are those times that circumstance jolts me back to a better balance.

We are all told to "hug our kids harder," "cherish those you love," "don't spend all your time working," and so on, but this particular morning, the clichés took on new meaning.

For the first time in 10 years, we are closing the day after Thanksgiving. I want my staff to be with people they love. I want them to spend time being with the people that they work so hard for all year long. I want their priority to be making memories and laughing. And loving.

I changed a lot of how I ran my business and the time I gave my staff off after that morning in 2013. I gave all my staff more opportunities for time off and started sending everyone home early on days that were close to holidays or so slow that there was no reason for them to be simply staring at their computer screen or waiting for the phone to ring. And I pay them for those hours when they're sent home before 5 p.m.

I want my staff to be at all their kids' school plays, baseball games, and swim meets. I want them to know that they can be there for their ailing parents and have a company that understands. I have learned that what people now value is that flexibility and time with their family and friends,

Figure 59.1 EIS staff and interpreters at a cultural parade

especially post-COVID. Give it to them. It works and is appreciated. It retains staff. There is nothing more costly to a company than a revolving door of employees.

CHAPTER 60

Putting on the Brakes

I had a good 15 years of working 70+ hour work weeks, and often covering 24/7 emergency calls. I felt that if I pushed to expand any further, I would lose any personal life altogether. I had built the business while working through the loss of my grandmother, mother-in-law, brother-in-law, and then my parents. I had gained weight, was not eating well, sleeping well, or taking care of myself physically, and the thought of growing the business any further was overwhelming.

Like many business owners, I was not a good delegator. I am a bit of a perfectionist and letting go of control is still something I struggle with daily. I had a huge life change around that 15-year mark. I left central New York, putting Syracuse behind and with a game plan to split my time between Philadelphia and Charlotte to be near my sons and their families.

The place in Charlotte I had purchased several years before this final move, so it was settled. However, the condo in Philly needed a lot of remodeling. I got to work quickly with renovations and found myself spending most of my time focused here. What I didn't plan on as I backed off my hours working and focused on settling in the City of Brotherly Love was that there wasn't much love here. I knew no one except my son and his wife. With my desire to lead a more balanced life, I started to think about how to become more physically healthy.

Walking around the neighborhood one day, I happened to pass by a small private gym and could see a young man training an older client through the window. I was a bit fascinated by the idea of private training sessions. Who wants to be overweight and work out around others? I could chew up some lonely hours by getting healthier. I walked in and left my contact information with Matt, the trainer I saw through the window and owner of Functionally Fit, two blocks from my condo in the Old City section of Philadelphia. And my life changed forever and for the better with that one chance meeting.

I worked out with Matt three times per week. At first, I hated my workouts. Was my stomach showing? Did I look ridiculous? Was anyone looking through that big picture window I had looked through weeks before? But Matt was very kind while really pushing hard. He repeatedly took my focus off my insecurities and onto each exercise we were doing. He was always so encouraging while holding me accountable. He was different from every other trainer I'd had, and I'd had a few over the years while trying to get in shape. Matt watched every move I made. He emphasized form in the gym, he emphasized cardio outside the gym, and he always asked for an account of what I was eating at home.

Being goal oriented and not wanting to let down my trainer, I stuck with it. For months. And then I saw huge results. It wasn't that I was losing so much weight, but I was going down size after size. I looked better in my clothes. I was stronger. I no longer felt embarrassed to be in the gym doing exercises and didn't worry about the people passing by. About that same time, I started talking more and more to my son in Philadelphia about running. He is an avid runner and has run ultramarathons. His words spurred me on: "Mom, if you can walk, you can jog. If you can jog, you can run."

And then the unthinkable happened. COVID happened. Unable to travel back and forth from Philly to Charlotte and trying to keep the business open and all my staff still employed, I decided to sell the place in Charlotte and use the proceeds to keep the business afloat. It was a heartbreaking decision as it meant time away from my family there. But it was the right decision for the business.

The isolation was setting in hard. But I was walking, then jogging, then running as my mental escape and promise to Matt to keep "getting in my cardio." Workouts were now virtual, and I purchased a treadmill so that I could run inside when the weather was bad outside. I ran a 5K, then a 7K, a 10K, and eventually a half-marathon. I had a very inflamed tendon by the half marathon and never ran more than 11 miles that day; however, I had run a full 13 miles while training. But I was now a runner. At this stage of my life, to say I had started over is an understatement.

The side effect was that I was pulling away from the business more and more. The staff were taking care of the day-to-day, and I was providing more oversight and was less "in the weeds" of what was going on.

I felt no qualms in putting my running and workouts as a priority. The year I ran the half-marathon I added Pilates to my schedule. I was finally committed to being a physically stronger person. And it gave me the confidence to be a stronger person at work.

I no longer worry about how I looked. I was wearing a size 8 and was a runner! I felt like I was finally in control of a huge part of my life. It was empowering. In my personal and business life, it made a huge difference in how I looked at myself.

I also took other care of myself. I went to an orthodontist and got Invisalign. Although I had always had straight teeth, I could see in Zoom meetings that my teeth were starting to "crowd." After a few months with Invisalign, I had my perfect smile again! This, along with regular visits to the hair salon, dermatologist, and nail salon, were giving me the confidence I needed. Remember the story about my clothes and how important your being a representation of your business is? Women especially get hung up on "this is all too self-indulgent" instead of "this is important for your business" along with your own physical and mental health.

Looking back, my mother rarely got her hair done. Never her nails. She never had a massage in her life or had her makeup done. She never had a personal trainer or wore high-end labeled clothes. I believe that, for herself, she felt those things were an indulgence and unnecessary. Almost embarrassing. That was her generation and the culture in which she lived. However, growing up, not seeing her ever do those things for herself had an influence. It was difficult for me to wrap my head around the fact that I was a representation of my business and need to take care of myself. As all business owners should.

Think about it this way: if you were going to meet your financial advisor or your banker, would you feel confident if you walked into their office to see them in disarray? Someone who obviously never took the time to take care of themselves? Or would you feel more confident shaking hands with someone who was put together in a fashion that showed they cared about their appearance and spent time to be a polished representative of their business?

CHAPTER 61

Stop Apologizing!

One thing I have not been good at over the last 20 years of being a business owner is setting boundaries, saying no, and apologizing for just about everything.

Recently, my CFO told me to "stop apologizing" in response to a situation where a customer was being unreasonable and the beginning of my e-mail back to her was, "I'm so sorry, but...." Bottom line, my CFO was right. I knew she had hit on something.

I pasted a digital sticky note to my desktop that said "stop apologizing" and began to really see how many times I'd been saying "I'm so sorry" when the asks were completely out of line. Whether business or personal, every single time I had to say no, I found myself apologizing. And it made me take a hard look at why.

I believe women are particularly vulnerable to feeling guilty when they set limits. I started to replace "I'm sorry" with "Unfortunately ..." and fill in the blanks. That wasn't much better. Instead of saying "I'm sorry, but our contract terms are…" I was saying "Unfortunately, our contract terms are ..."

I needed to go further. I replaced the first sticky with a second: "STOP saying 'unfortunately.'"

So today I smiled when a customer bemoaned conditions in a contract they had signed. I began my e-mail with, "On page 2 of our agreement it clearly states our cancellation policy. If you need a copy of the contract, I'm happy to send it over." No apology. No "unfortunately." I'm still learning!

CHAPTER 62

Mental Health and Entrepreneurship

I read with great sadness, however without surprise, that a successful young entrepreneur and business owner recently committed suicide by jumping to her death off an NYC high-rise. It was the first time I have seen the issue of mental health and entrepreneurship being discussed. However, she would not be the first startup founder to commit suicide.

Many people may think that a CEO may be taking their life because of tax problems, a failing business, or other major company issues. That is not the case. As reported on the Facebook page of The Academi of Life, "Suicides can be a result of battling depression, which can be exacerbated by the stress of starting a company." A study by Dr. Michael Freeman, a clinical professor at the University of California, San Francisco, and an entrepreneur, was one of the first to link higher rates of mental-health issues to entrepreneurship.

Of the 242 entrepreneurs he surveyed, 49 percent reported having a mental-health condition. Depression was the number one reported condition among them and was present in 30 percent of all entrepreneurs, followed by anxiety problems at 27 percent. That's a much higher percentage than the U.S. population at large, where about 7 percent identify as depressed.

As a founder and business owner, I know the toll running the day-to-day can take. "The buck stops here" is a constant and there is no escaping. From one problem employee to one unhappy customer, it wears on you. Even the successes and business growth can be grueling. It can be wonderful, and it can be horrific.

The bottom line is we need to be aware and take care of our bodies *and* minds. Having a support system of others running businesses is imperative. Alone time to destress is crucial. And time with *only* family and loved ones is paramount. It will get to you, not just the taxes, the new regulations, the endless meetings. The day-to-day will get to you. A word of caution: Take care. Take good care. Put a plan of action in place and keep yourself in check. I have an advisor I can call at any time, and she walks me through the dark times when I'm not sure where to turn. I have a Bible nearby to ground me. I have a box of family photos in a desk drawer to remind me why I do what I do. And I have an e-mail box labeled "When I'm feeling overwhelmed" which is full of thank you notes from customers, interpreters, and consumers that help me get through the stress.

Whatever works for you, find that support. NO business is worth falling into a despair that you cannot climb out of. Mental health and entrepreneurship is a topic worth discussing.

CHAPTER 63

Fingerprints on the Window

As I wrote my last chapter on mental health and leading a business, I was reminded of wisdom from the two most influential women in my life. Something my mother always said *and* the most memorable story my grandmother had ever told me: The fingerprints on the window.

"This too shall pass" was my Mother's favorite saying, no matter how bad things seemed. She believed that, one way or another, the issue at hand will be resolved. And only the permanent in life and the people in our lives were what really mattered. This memory from my mother was to be the first half of my lesson.

The second was the sobering story my grandmother had told me.

Grandma was the eternal optimist. I saw it until the absolute end of her 99 years on Earth. And I honestly wondered how, knowing she had lost two children as a very young mother—a daughter at age six, her son just a toddler of two. She had told me the story of losing her little girl and only a short year later her tousled hair baby boy. She told of how he would toddle to the old wooden windows that hung low enough in their house that he could reach the windowpanes on his own. He would make handprints when it rained, where warmth met cold, and he could play on his tablet of glass. His favorite place in their little apartment.

Her lesson to me, at the time, was to learn that by trying to control things and make them better, we often make them worse. In this story, it was her mother-in-law. By the time my grandmother had lost her second child, she was left literally speechless and in a dark hole of sorrow. Her mother-in-law had been summoned to come stay to offer comfort and temporarily take over the household. The visit was ended, and punctuated with horror, when my grandmother came out of her bedroom one morning to touch the pane of glass that still held little Benjamin's fingerprints, only to discover they had been wiped away by the hand of his grandmother, trying to remove a memory she thought would be painful to her daughter-in-law. This only cracked my grandmother's soul once again as she realized those precious fingerprints were gone forever.

What it reminded me of today is that the bad, the stress, the unknowns in life are not what should matter. It is the people that we love. Who will not always be here. The family, the memories. The fingerprints we hold onto. Stop trying to control events as you can easily make things worse. Because inevitably, *"this too shall pass."*

CHAPTER 64

"When I Feel Overwhelmed"

Before my business was "born" and I was devouring every book on entrepreneurship at Barnes & Noble, I was struck by a remark from one billionaire business owner. He talked about how he grounded himself with a drawer full of reminders as to why he was doing what he was doing. When he wanted to quit, when staff issues or contract negotiations were stressing him to the point of wanting to sell his business, he would look in the bottom drawer in his desk. In that drawer were all the reasons he should, and would, keep going. Pictures of his kids. Thank you notes from employees, customers, and the charities he supported.

One by one, they reminded him of why he worked so hard, why he gave his life to his company. With all the naysayers that will breathe down your neck, you will need a drawer of reasons why you do what you do. Those reasons will not be awards you have won or a banner fiscal year. It will be the people. It will be the impact you make. Whether it's making your family member's life better because you can help them out or because you worked hard to make a difference with a customer. I knew I would need a drawer full of reminders by my first year in business.

My "drawer" is a Gmail file I put to the side and labeled "When I'm overwhelmed." It is from that file that I pull out and read meaningful, encouraging words. There are always pictures of my family in there and on my screensaver. I'd like to share a few examples here.

From two different interpreters we mentored:

"Thank you for working so hard for me and all your employees. I know we can't imagine the amount of dedication and effort that goes into enabling all of us to live the lives we do. It means a lot to me." "I want to thank you for your love and support. I am grateful for you, your kindness, and your listening ear. I will never forget that you have been there every step of the way. It means

a lot to me more than you can imagine. I am truly blessed. I just want you to know how much I appreciate you."

From a previous employee:

"I just wanted to send you a quick thank you note. I recently signed a contract to translate a book with a small publishing house in France that is trying to break one of their authors into the US-English market. I know that there is no version of me getting to this point without my time with you and at EIS."

Current employee:

"Thank you so much ... you mean so much to me, you have no idea!"

Current interpreter:

"I am deeply thankful for all the opportunities you have sent my way and still send my way. You remain in my mind as a person of highest integrity, a phenomenal businesswoman and a treasured friend. Let's keep looking forward together to a bright future!"

A local businesswoman:

"I just wanted to reach out and say CONGRATULATIONS for being honored as April's SWM cover woman! You have personally inspired me from the day I met you. Thank you for all that you do in this community, through your business, your entrepreneurial spirit, and your general awesomeness! Simply amazing."

From my hairdresser and her daughter who were marching to fight breast cancer:

"Today we walked, we walked for you. You're not only a survivor, but you are also an inspiration. You truly are one of the best, brilliant, strongest, most wonderfully successful woman I know. You're a beacon of strength and inspiration to all women."

CHAPTER 65

I Did Not Come This Far to Only Come This Far

So where are Empire Interpreting Service and the language service industry in general at this point, and what lies in our future? Twenty years ago, we changed the way LSPs were being run and what the offerings were across New York State. Today, the industry is influencing and changing what our individual businesses look like now and what they will look like in the future.

AI is certainly beginning to redefine our industry. COVID pushed forward virtual interpreting, which I can honestly say goes against my innermost being as I know an onsite, in-person interpreter is always the best. However, I understand there is a place for technology, whether in an emergency or when there is no interpreter available for a specific language pairing. Unfortunately, I have seen customers choose virtual or telephonic interpreting strictly because of the cost savings. Our consumers are the ones that suffer.

Can you imagine having a baby or being given a grim diagnosis via an app on someone's phone or a faceless voice that comes through a speaker? Taking the human element out of the equation leaves our consumers who do not speak English or are deaf more isolated than ever and questioning the quality of what and who is interpreting.

I believe now it is our responsibility as owners of LSPs to educate and remind customers of their common goals with the people they serve. And give them all options available to make it more comfortable and as seamless as possible, ensuring that both sides are receiving quality and competent language access. It is a new and looming part of the future and one that will take a lot of balancing.

My personal goal is to keep the tenets I built the business on: of providing highly vetted and skilled interpreters and excellent customer service to all involved while still moving into the future. Much like languages are constantly changing, so are our businesses. The challenge now is to learn and embrace change while we hold fast to our ethics and practices. I believe the time I leave the industry will be when I feel that can no longer happen.

When I depart Empire Interpreting Service, and I will someday, I will be proud of what we accomplished. We raised the bar on what interpreting services looked like in the areas that we served. We vetted our interpreters at a higher standard than had ever been done before. We had better customer service, and it was 24/7/365. We were there for our interpreters. *They* set their rates, not us, which is proper for 1099 subcontractors. We paid them on schedule and on time. We provided support to them by making sure they had the information and prep needed to do their jobs. These were all things I saw lacking in the field when I was a freelancer. I can look back now and be proud of what we have provided in our industry.

However, what is most satisfying is what happened with my staff. I have been able to pay higher than industry standard to each staff. They all receive four weeks paid vacation and a week of personal time. Our maternity and paternity leave allowed both my sons to have extended time home with their children and another key staff member multiple months home with her son. I make sure to rarely say no to time off requests. I am purposely flexible when it comes to any staff wanting time off to be with family. I know that policy for staff makes a difference in the lives of their children, and hopefully to their extended family as well.

Back to My 15-Year-Old Self

I refer to myself at 15 years old often when I talk about my business because our lives are building blocks and our experiences mold who we are and what we become. I believe the desperation in just being able to survive day-to-day, month-to-month, and year-to-year has greatly shaped my life and how I run my business.

My hope is that I can learn that elusive comfort of being outside of your business and leaning hard into the joys of life, of being with family and friends, and experiencing the peace of the day-to-day outside my company. Street smarts and hard work can and did push me toward a successful business. My next goal is to learn how to feel okay when not driving so hard—maybe to regain some of the unbridled joy of being a teenager and make up for a multitude of lost years.

When you go through life with the motivation of hunger or making sure you have a roof over your head, or protecting yourself and your child from violence, it can be almost impossible to stop once you don't need to worry about those things anymore. When you see those signs of success finally come to fruition, the idea of it disappearing is terrifying. Work is my comfort zone. Relaxation and backing off is not. However, I see it coming. I see the need to reap the benefits as the years continue to march on and time runs out.

About the Author

Theresa Slater, author of *The Language of Success,* grew up in the small town in upstate New York with virtually no diversity in her school or community, where everyone spoke the same language and looked monochromatic. Fast forward to today; she is the founder and owner of Empire Interpreting Service, a language service providing company that provides interpreters and translators in hundreds of languages.

Theresa now lives in the midst of multiple cultures and language users, in the historic center of Philadelphia, Old City. Her life now filled with opportunities abound, she has found a love for the city and explores its richness through art museums, theater, and music. While embracing all Philly has to offer, she's also become an avid runner and fitness buff. When she's not exploring the city around her, she is drinking in as much time as she can with her family and friends.

Index

OTHER TITLES IN THE BUSINESS CAREER DEVELOPMENT COLLECTION

Vilma Barr, Consultant, Editor

- *Make Your Internship Count* by Marti Fischer
- *Sales Excellence* by Eden White
- *How to Think Strategically* by Greg Githens
- *Succeeding as a Young Entrepreneur* by Harvey Morton
- *The Intentional Mindset* by Jane Frankel
- *Still Room for Humans* by Stan Schatt
- *Am I Doing This Right?* by Tony D. Thelen, Matthew C. Mitchell and Jeffrey A. Kappen
- *Telling Your Story, Building Your Brand* by Henry Wong
- *Social Media Is About People* by Cassandra Bailey and Dana M. Schmidt
- *Pay Attention!* by Cassandra M. Bailey and Dana M. Schmidt
- *Remaining Relevant* by Karen Lawson
- *The Road to Champagne* by Alejandro Colindres Frañó
- *Burn Ladders. Build Bridges* by Alan M. Patterson
- *Decoding Your STEM Career* by Peter J Devenyi
- *The Networking Playbook* by Darryl Howes

Concise and Applied Business Books

The Collection listed above is one of 30 business subject collections that Business Expert Press has grown to make BEP a premiere publisher of print and digital books. Our concise and applied books are for...

- Professionals and Practitioners
- Faculty who adopt our books for courses
- Librarians who know that BEP's Digital Libraries are a unique way to offer students ebooks to download, not restricted with any digital rights management
- Executive Training Course Leaders
- Business Seminar Organizers

Business Expert Press books are for anyone who needs to dig deeper on business ideas, goals, and solutions to everyday problems. Whether one print book, one ebook, or buying a digital library of 110 ebooks, we remain the affordable and smart way to be business smart. For more information, please visit www.businessexpertpress.com, or contact sales@businessexpertpress.com.

www.ingramcontent.com/pod-product-compliance
Lightning Source LLC
Chambersburg PA
CBHW061315220326
41599CB00026B/4892